THE ANATOMY
OF SILENCE

Praise for *The Anatomy of Silence*

"A powerful, painful and brilliant collection of stories,
the perfect reminder of why we need change
and why we need it now."
Rebecca Reid, Journalist and author, Perfect Liars

★

"To read this book is to fully witness the world we live
in, a world where sexual violence can abscond and replicate
in part due to our silence. *The Anatomy of Silence* is a
bursting, creative, courageous puncture of that silence, a
beacon for something so much more."
*Jess Mack, Vice President for Strategy and
Communications, Global Health Corps*

★

"A vitally important project for our age. A compelling read
that proves how the fusion of art, speaking out, and sharing
truth are the keys to transforming a broken culture."
*Dr. Jamie Marich, best-selling author of
six books on trauma recovery*

★

"This is a book full of details. Of ambivalence. Of uncertainties. Of realities. You will learn something by reading it; mostly you will feel something. Each story bristles with the emergence of a voice: someone telling, often for the first time, an account of what they carry in every cell of their body but you would never know about... because their voice was silenced long ago. This powerful collection of voices gather to form a cry: of freedom, grief, joy, and hope."
Emily Click, Assistant Dean for
Ministry Studies, Harvard Divinity School

★

"A pivotal step in combating sexual violence and the apathy and ignorance that is perpetuated by the current political climate. The stories in this book exemplify the courage, wisdom, intuition and strength necessary to use our voices and ask the necessary questions. We should all be so brave."
Suzi Rutti (MSW, LISW-S)
Social worker and trauma therapist

★

"Brutally honest and harrowing from the very first page. A reminder of how far we have come—and how much more there's left to do. There's so much that's unsaid, unnoticed, and untaught about sexual assault. This book calls an end to it. Now."
Emmie Harrison, Journalist (Metro)

"There's really no such thing as the 'voiceless'. There are only the deliberately silenced, or the preferably unheard."

–Arundhati Roy

"Every social justice movement that I know of has come out of people sitting in small groups, telling their life stories, and discovering that other people have shared similar experiences."

–Gloria Steinem

"There are very few human beings who receive the truth, complete and staggering, by instant illumination. Most of them acquire it fragment by fragment... by successive developments... like a laborious mosaic."

–Anaïs Nin

THE ANATOMY OF SILENCE

TWENTY-SIX STORIES ABOUT ALL THE SHIT THAT GETS IN THE WAY OF TALKING ABOUT SEXUAL VIOLENCE

edited by cyra perry dougherty

red press

Red Press
The Anatomy of Silence

Kresich, Joan. "Flying Out of Bed" Reprinted with permission from
Ms. Magazine Blog. 16 February 2018.
Bowdler, Michelle. "The Surprise that Surprises No One" Reprinted
with permission from *WordPeace Literary Journal*, Issue 2.3, Summer/
Fall 2018.
Marx, Frederick. "Men's Work" adapted from *At Death Do Us Part.*
Oakland: Warrior Films, August 2018.

Edited by Cyra Perry Dougherty
Cover design Katherine Knotts
Printed in the USA by Versa Press (Chicago)
Typeset in Bembo

Published by Red Press
ISBN 978 1 912157 105 (Paperback)
ISBN 978 1 912157 112 (Ebook)

A catalogue record for this book is available from the British Library

Red Press Registered Offices:
6 Courtenay Close, Wareham, Dorset, BH20 4ED, England
www.redpress.co.uk
@redpresspub

#CanYouHearTheSilence

Content Warning

Our book is about the culture of silence surrounding sexual violence.

Our book is unapologetically loud.

The content of this book will be emotionally challenging to read at times—and first and foremost we want you to take care of yourself. But here's the thing: we are writing about the hard stuff so that we can find ways of talking about the hard stuff. We can't talk about ending the culture of silence surrounding sexual violence without talking about the nature of the violence itself—whether in the form of creative expression, first-person narratives, or aggregated statistics. This book is about making sure we break the silence once and for all. This is a book about changing the culture that perpetuates silence—because it's the silence that allows the violence to thrive, and even to exist in the first place. Talking about it is the first step on the road towards healing.

Do whatever you need to do to read this book. Skip chapters. Dip in and out. Take it one paragraph at a time. Breathe. Talk about it. Write about it. We're in this together.

Contents

Introduction
Cyra Perry Dougherty

"LA VIOLÓ! LA VIOLÓ!" Her voice came through like bullets as I stood holding the phone, which was tethered to the night stand by a too-short cord. I couldn't move—couldn't even bring myself to sit down on the bed.

He raped her. No—he just violated her. Nope—that word means rape. My mind spun as I tried to accurately translate her words—so clear yet so inexact when outside my native tongue.

At first I thought it was important to understand exactly what she was saying—to understand the precise degree to which he had taken advantage of her—but I soon realized it was not important at all. The woman shouting on the phone was communicating something horrific to me. Quibbling in my mind over translations was not helpful. Here's what mattered: he had done something awful.

He was my son's father. I had just turned 22 and was living with him in a small one bedroom in Santiago, Chile—his hometown. Diego was barely six months old. The tension in our home was growing by the day as the monster of his addiction spewed despair, violence, and rage upon anything and everything it met. The pain of our suffering as a family was enough. And now I was living with a rapist? He violated a young 18-year-old girl in her own home. It sounded like he broke into the house. *But maybe not.* It sounded like something out of my nightmares. *But maybe it wasn't.* I couldn't read between the lines. He had been partying until early in the morning with the girl's father. *I think.* The person on the other end of the phone line was that man's wife, the girl's mother. *Definitely.*

Given the tumult of life with him, it was hard to be surprised by the phone call. Yet still, every ounce of my being felt tortured by the voice on the phone, as if I were being held up to the fire, forced to stand there burning. He'd been gone for nearly two days. He was on a cocaine-fueled binge. Clearly what this woman was saying held truth—I had no doubt. But was this my responsibility? What was I supposed to do for this woman, for her daughter? What did she want me to do?

Doing her best to hurl the responsibility for this incident in my direction, this suffering mother seemed caught off-guard when, in as calm a voice as I could muster, I responded: *Usted necesita llamar a los pacos. Lo siento mucho. Lo que ha pasado es terrible. Pero yo no puedo controlarlo. No sé que puedo hacer. No puedo controlarlo.* She needed to call the police. I'm sorry. What happened is terrible. I can't control him. I don't know what I can do. I can't control him.

It's all I could think of.

I was drawing the line.

I could not fix this.

Perhaps surprised that I was not leaping to protect my boyfriend; shocked that I suggested law enforcement; stunned by my foreign accent; recognizing the pain in my voice – I'm not sure – but suddenly she changed her tone. She dialed back her anger. Asked if I was okay. I told her about his addiction. She told me her husband was sober, had struggled with addiction for a long time—and that with the right help, things could change for us. It was difficult not to laugh or scoff at this idea. Her husband hanging with my boyfriend was not a good sign for his sobriety. What's more, as her anger subsided, she seemed to be letting the man who so painfully violated her daughter off the hook for what, moments before, was an unforgivable incident of sexual violence in need of swift action on my part. What had happened? What kinds of alternate realities were we jumping between? I needed her to be angry. I needed her to speak out—but I needed her to tell someone else, someone who could help. Not knowing what else to do, I reminded her to call the police (frankly, I felt I was begging her to), and I hung up the phone.

It was like being dropped into one of those 'choose your own adventure' books: selecting the 'call the police' page thrust me into a whole new world—where the focus of the story shifted from this woman and her daughter's trauma to my own. To the story of my relationship with this suffering, struggling, traumatized, violent, shame-filled, addicted, charismatic, charming man whom I had chosen to have a child with, to live with, to love. I was caught off guard and yet somewhere I knew that all these narratives were interwoven in the same book.

RAPE WAS NOT A NEW TOPIC FOR ME. As the statistics show, survivors of sexual violence are more likely to experience it – and other forms of domestic and intimate partner violence – again. That was me, apparently.

Three years earlier – elsewhere – I was raped after a date with a man I'd met in a bar a few nights earlier. We had agreed to share a cab home. The cab driver was going to drop him first. But once we arrived at his house, a neighborhood I didn't know, he coaxed me out of the cab. The driver ignored my requests to be taken back to my apartment—first with silence and then with a swift foot on the gas as my date managed to close the car door with one hand while pulling me out with the other.

Did I miss something?

Did I miscommunicate?

We entered my date's apartment. I'd already gone into shock. I don't remember speaking a single word after entering that apartment. It felt as if I were watching a movie of myself. I knew what was coming, but I couldn't stop it from playing out on the screen. All I could do was to silently root for my survival.

We passed a Scandinavian woman sitting on the couch painting her toenails, her boyfriend wandering around the living room. What must that moment have looked like to them as we walked up the stairs and into his bedroom? What about the moment, not long after, that I hurried out of the bedroom and searched for a way out of the apartment?

My memory of the moments in between is that I watched from the upper corner of the bedroom as he used and manipulated my body for his pleasure. I'm sure this distancing, movie-watcher effect is my brain offering me some type of powerful protective force. To this day, the feeling of being separated from my body creates a hard-to-explain barrier between me and the pain of the experience—a kind of a disbelief, sometimes a deep silence.

THIS IS ALL TO SAY, three years later, when I received that phone call, rumination about rape was familiar to me.

I was familiar with the oscillation between a fierce conviction that I had been wronged and a wondering if it could really be called 'rape'. In my moments of doubt, I was sure I didn't do enough to fight, to resist, to speak forcefully.

I was well-versed in questioning whether an outside observer would have known what I felt; whether the cab driver or the woman painting her toenails could see what was happening; whether they willfully ignored my need for help.

Listening to the woman on the phone, I was thrown back into this old familiar story—but I was seeing it from another perspective. This time, I was aligned with the assaulter. It was notably less familiar territory for me—but the critical, judgmental voice in my head was the same. *Could it have really been rape? What actually happened? If I had seen it would it have been obvious? What would I have done if I had been there? Who was the girl? What was her father doing?*

The memory of what happened next is distant, fleeting, perhaps non-existent in any coherent form. The snapshots – fragments – from those days elude any clear timeline in my mind. A mirror was punched. There was blood. Phone ripped out of my hand, thrown off the balcony. Yelling. Crying—a baby crying. The pain, the anger—they defied language then, and still do. It is a terrifying boiling, a burning, in my body that makes me wonder what horrible thing I might be capable of.

This fragmentation, this feeling, this inability to string words together—that's what trauma does to us.

That was over fourteen years ago. Not long afterwards, I left Chile.

FOR YEARS, I DIDN'T TALK ABOUT MY LIFE THERE. Much like I had spent years not talking about the rape. I was ashamed. I felt stupid. I knew I'd be judged for inviting these people into my life. I was so smart—how could I let anyone see me as dumb, as weak? I'd been taught that you could prevent rape and domestic violence by being smart, by making the right choices. If you make the right choices—it will all be fine. But make the wrong choices—beware.

Therapy, Al-Anon, spiritual practices, and above all a fierce commitment to motherhood have led me on a slow, winding path of healing. As I gained distance from the relationship with Diego's father, the shame of loving someone so violent subsided, and the confusion of grieving the loss of a relationship that hurt me so badly softened.

By developing a sense of self that was separate from the stories of my past, I was able to manage the shame. I began to talk more about what had happened to me. I found that my most honest healing conversations involved talking about both the rape and my life with Diego's father. Processing the connections between those experiences helped me understand how my shame and silence about the rape shaped the way I approached relationships: overlooking red flags, willfully denying reality, turning to silence, and reactivating shame.

In recent years, I have talked a lot about these experiences in detail—in writing, speaking, and with family and friends. Managing the shame I carried – and still carry – and figuring out ways to accept and speak about being both a victim and a survivor has deeply informed my understanding of the work of both spiritual healing and social justice.

But I have never, until working on this book, told the story of that phone call. And I hadn't ever considered what my fear of disclosing that phone call to others meant until I was confronted with a much deeper question: *where do our silences surrounding sexual violence come from, and how are they perpetuated?*

That question, and the seed of the idea for this book, was planted in October 2016. Following the release of the video of the Donald Trump 'locker room' chat with Billy Bush about 'grabbing women by the pussy', I was confronted with that boiling, burning, body-held-to-the-fire feeling again. By that time, I'd spent years developing the skills to navigate such feelings without turning to self-blame, to rage, or to fear—and most importantly, I had learned to talk about sexual violence.

I could hear the truth in both Trump's candor and denial. There was no doubt in my mind that he had abused women in the ways he described. I spent the better part of a day crafting a Facebook post that would explain my disgust, call out the culture of violence Trump had been cultivating in his campaign, and make me feel empowered in the face of the painful memories – and all of my associated physical and emotional reactions – his words provoked. In an expansive post, I suggested that Trump's tactics of feigned apology, denial, blaming, shaming, fear-mongering, and normalizing are the specific behaviors of abusers everywhere.

Though Trump is certainly not the first man in power to act this way, it enraged me to see all of those behaviors – ones that therapy taught me to identify as abusive, manipulative, and red flags in relationships – enacted so plainly by this man running for the highest office.

My heart hurt to think of the millions of traumatized people across America, who have yet to begin the painful, often expensive, and always time-consuming healing process, who would be held hostage to his tactics and react much in the ways that battered partners do—minimizing the behavior, avoiding the topic, silencing themselves, and trying to preserve a sense of normality at all costs.

In an instant, Trump had become yet another living case study about the ways an abuser (and a system writ large) can leverage our culture of shame to encourage, or insist upon, silence in cases of sexual violence.

As the months passed, I watched my son Diego navigate middle school and try to make meaning of Trump, sexism, and what he believed about the world. I worried a lot about my ability to raise a different kind of man. I also finished my third trimester of pregnancy—my baby girl was born just weeks before hundreds of thousands of women marched for their voices and rights on inauguration day in January 2017. Lying in the hospital bed next to my loving, gentle husband, I wondered if my baby girl and I would make it to the march. I prayed that she wouldn't have to suffer in the ways I have, in the ways so many of us have. And I realized that something bigger than Trump was at play. Trump was merely a symptom of a larger problem—a historic, socially-embedded violence that so many of us simply try to ignore.

As a mother, a woman, a citizen of the United States, I was desperate to understand how so many in our country could look away from the stark reality of Trump's hate and violence; how it could simply be a non-issue; how it could cease to exist as a factor in their analysis of his suitability for leadership. This desperation mirrored my obsession with trying to understand why the cab driver ignored me, how the Scandinavian woman continued painting her toenails rather than acknowledging what was unfolding in her home. *How could people just let this happen? Am I the only one seeing this?*

Later, as the #MeToo movement spread like wildfire in my social media feeds, it became clear I was not alone. Far too many of us have lived in silence—struggling to understand how people could look away, ignore our suffering, coerce us to stop talking, and solve their own discomfort by shaming and blaming us.

I said #MeToo—but I was scared that it wouldn't make a damn bit of difference. That once again we'd be heard for a moment and then promptly forgotten. That our voices would have only a fleeting impact before people returned to their normal lives. That our stories wouldn't change the culture we're immersed in, and therefore the political, social, economic, and religious systems that we create to govern our lives and choices would forcefully protect the status quo. That we would never recognize how, through our silences, we are all complicit in creating a world where sexual violence is pandemic.

I took to social media again, this time with a post soliciting proposals for essays that could speak to the culture of silence surrounding sexual violence. With that, *The Anatomy of Silence* was conceived.

The energy, ideas, and connections unleashed by that post held me accountable to moving forward with the project. As people's stories trickled in, it became clear that embedded in the tangled mess of our stories about silence surrounding sexual violence were key insights on how our collective silences operate within a larger culture of shame—a culture of shushing and blaming and objectifying and judging and protecting the status quo. It turns out that silence, and the shame it thrives in, are largely created by the choices we make everyday about how we engage with and respond to others.

Yet as I grew more committed to and inspired by the project, the weight of responsibility that I felt for stewarding people's stories into this book caused me to go deeply inward—to a place that felt too vulnerable to share with anyone. I was overwhelmed by the number of stories of childhood sexual abuse that I received. I was pained by the ways we internalize cues from family, institutions, and the world around us about what is not acceptable or appropriate to do or say. I suffered with those still carrying untreated wounds so very long after experiencing sexual violence. I was baffled by stories of how the systems designed to protect us so often fail us. I was moved to tears by the ways so many of us have to fight for healing and voice. None of this was new to me, but once again, it all seemed like too much to talk about.

Part of me rationalized my inward turn as 'meditative'—and in many ways, it was. Turning inward allowed me to take care of myself, to not be subject to the demands, questions, or judgments of others, to not place too much attention on the performance or the product of this book. And yet, the inward turn began to feel a lot like the silences I kept in the years following my rape and relationship with Diego's father—self-protective but filled with fear, isolation, and the murky waters of shame.

Six months into the project, with deadlines passing unmet, I realized my silence about the book was, fundamentally, an attempt to avoid pain. Realizing that holding my breath through the rest of project would lead to suffocation, I confessed it to my therapist and some colleagues. I slowly began to share that I was working on the project and how difficult it had been. My energy shifted, and I no longer felt so alone in carrying it forward.

My silence about this book was not a coincidence. I still deeply fear judgment, victim-blamers, minimizers, and other critics; I fear those who are unable to bear listening to our stories—to accept hearing the ways that their beliefs, actions, or comments may have silenced people; I fear those who will fight the changes they realize they need to make; I fear those who will turn their backs on us again. These are not fears born out of my anxiety and imagination—these are fears born out of direct experience and witness. Fears born out of the times I've been told to toughen up or stop asking for a fight. Fears born out of seeing the most public of silence-breakers blamed, shamed, shunned and smeared—from Anita Hill to Christine Blasey Ford.

It was in acknowledging the reality of these fears that I remembered the story of that phone call so many years ago in my Santiago apartment. I recalled the feeling of being held to the fire, of receiving a woman's rage, of the sense that I was being asked to take responsibility for what happened to her daughter.

I wondered if, for some, #MeToo feels like a never-ending string of those calls. There's a trauma involved in having your worldview upended, in not knowing what to do, or where to turn when you hear stories of other people's suffering. How much of the common pattern of denial, shame, blame, and silence is simply a coping mechanism to avoid accepting the painful truth that there is sexual violence in our world? How much will healing and justice be contingent on us all confronting our fears, whether they are of sharing or of believing?

As I finalized the proofs for this book, as if the world were calling forth its message, Christine Blasey Ford testified courageously before the Senate, Brett Kavanaugh doubled down on his denial, conservative talking heads and typing hands launched their campaigns to discredit Ford's message and normalize Kavanaugh's behavior, and survivors everywhere explained publicly (as a rebuttal to Trump's denial and gaslighting) the very painful reasons why they did not report the sexual violence that happened to them.

We explained how damn traumatizing it is to hear others dismiss our stories. How the violation of not being heard, of not being believed, mirrors the pain of the sexual violence itself. How it amplifies the experiences in which our voices, our "No's", our "Please Don'ts", our "Stops", our signals and signs of discomfort were ignored. We kept silent because those who hurt us can (and so often do) simply deny, lie, and dismiss our words as fantasy—and because data shows that the world is much more comfortable believing that it didn't happen (at least not as we describe it) than that it did.

Yet accepting that it did happen, accepting that it does happen, opens the door to another, potentially even more painful and divisive conversation: What do we do now? What does meaningful justice look like? How do healing and justice relate? And what work do we need to do at a cultural, social, and political level to ensure that we can heal, find justice, and make sure that sexual violence ends? On the day that Kavanaugh was ultimately sworn in, on the day he took up the mantle of shaping how 'justice' is defined in my country, it occurred to me that, like Trump, he was merely a symptom of a larger problem—call it white male supremacy, empire culture, the American Dream; call it fear, insecurity, or the search for belonging, worth, and value in an oppressive society; call it any and all of these things, they all run deeper than any one person.

We have a lot of work to do. All of that work starts with being able to tell our stories and being able to listen to the stories of others. Based on the numbers alone, each one of us knows a survivor, and likely a perpetrator too—so we have ample opportunity to learn how to talk about sexual violence in truthful, healing, and respectful ways. Ways that open the door for conversations about imagining a different future. For instance, how would it have felt, what would it have changed in the public discourse if Kavanaugh had said *I don't know. I don't remember. I drank too much as a teen. I'm sorry if I hurt you.*

THE MEMORY OF HOW that terrible phone call felt – alongside the stories of the courageous survivors and allies who have contributed to this collection – has taught me that lasting social change lies on the other side of our collective healing work. We must heal from the ways that sex, shame, violence, racism, sexism, homophobia, toxic masculinity, bureaucracy, power, and silence have hurt us. This work will be daunting and painful for everyone. It will require us all (not only survivors) to connect to our pain, to be vulnerable to one another, to be accountable to one another, and to trust in ourselves and others. This kind of connecting is not going to be easy.

Trauma broke my ability to be in relationships—my silence allowed me to deny that I needed or deserved caring people to love me. We live in a traumatized world. Our unhealthy reactions to chronic stress and our deep desire to not feel our pain keep us collectively disconnected. This sounds stark. And it is. Healing requires us to connect and be in relationships—those of us who have been hurt by people need the caring support of someone's presence and love to redevelop trust. I believe we can all offer that to one another if we try. But sexual violence is everywhere, all around us. Our children, our siblings, our neighbors and colleagues, we are all in this mess together. If we can't find ways to encourage everyone to talk about it – the detailed, complex, hard-to-handle reality of it – and if we can't find ways to listen even when we don't have the power to rewind the tape and change the story we are hearing, we will perpetuate the trauma and hurt. We will allow those who have hurt people to deny their responsibility, evade accountability, and avoid atonement. We will destroy yet another generation's faith in the possibility of being protected from violence. And sexual violence will continue to go unchecked.

The stories that follow are searing, heart-wrenching, inspiring, and true examinations of the myriad ways we, all of us, learn to use silence. Within the experiences and insights shared here are contradictions and paradoxes worth exploring. There is not just one story but twenty-six—it is by accepting them all that we will find our way to understanding the inner and outer workings of our silences. Perhaps it is in such understanding that we find our voices, seek healing, and turn ourselves toward the work of justice—a fierce, loving justice that transforms the culture of shame, violence, and silence that we have come to accept.

I think of the other women who my son's father has hurt—it devastates me to accept that I couldn't prevent their suffering. It devastates me also that I couldn't heal his pain, which is what was needed to prevent him from hurting others. I don't believe I'll ever know the extent of his pain, or whether he deliberately intended to hurt others. I'm not sure it even matters. But I do believe – from the minor disclosures, the small comments, the glimpses of vulnerability through the clouds of his own silence – that he, too, was a victim of sexual violence. While being a victim cannot excuse his actions—his experience demands that we look more deeply at the impact of culturally-ingrained silences that allow shame to fester, and that facilitate further sexual violence. His story matters too. And in the question of how we move toward justice, finding ways to solicit and listen to stories like his will be essential.

I think about the woman on the phone, how quickly her tone changed. Maybe she was startled by the deep suffering she heard in my voice, the realization that her daughter and I had more in common than not? Maybe she was surprised at my willingness to believe her? Maybe she actually modeled the listening that we all need to do better when talking to someone in pain? Maybe she helped me to look at my own story and my own silences differently? And maybe she did the same for her daughter? She was the first – and the only person for many years – with whom I ever shared how out of control my life with him was. I was only able to do that because of the space she made – amidst her own anger and suffering – to listen to and connect with me.

Somehow all of our stories, as survivors, perpetrators, allies, witnesses, citizens of the world, are connected through the spiritual, cultural, political and social fabric of our coexistence—a cluttered pile of pages with no single, crisp, clear narrative or solution. No matter how complex and difficult it may be, I believe that by making meaning out of these collected stories, we will be able listen more deeply for the wounds that others carry. We will be able to hear silences differently. We will learn how to respond to suffering.

How to not look away. We will be given the opportunity to listen to our shame, to our anger. Listen to it—don't run away from it. We will be presented with the choice to talk more freely and gently about sex, feelings, intimacy, and our bodies. We will be offered an opportunity to explore forgiveness. We will have the opportunity to hold others accountable and also to be held accountable for our actions and inactions. And if we rise to the occasion, we will begin to heal together. Perhaps in doing so, we will re-imagine a future that does not repeat the mistakes of the past.

I desperately want to dismantle the cultural, social, political, and economic systems, structures, and institutions that protect the status quo. At times, I day-dream of a violent overthrow, and yet, my heart knows that the most radical transformation of our societies will only happen if I am able to live into my belief in and honor of the human dignity of each and every person on this planet—even those who have done great harm. From that place of faith in and love of our shared humanity, together I hope that we can effectively call for accountability and acknowledgment of the wrongs. I know that this will require those of us who are survivors and allies to contemplate forgiveness and those of us who have perpetrated harm to seek it. I lean on Archbishop Desmond Tutu's wisdom here and hope you will too as you read this book. Sexual violence is so pandemic that a retributive model of justice is likely not possible—we must seek out restorative models. Restorative, not in the sense of returning to something that was or preserving institutions as they were, but in the sense of restoring human dignity and connection in the face of suffering, violence, and disconnection.

In Tutu's words, "Forgiveness doesn't mean pretending things aren't as they really are. Forgiveness is recognition that there is a ghastliness that has happened. Forgiveness doesn't mean trying to paper over the cracks. Forgiveness means that both the wronged and the culprits of those wrongs acknowledge that something happened. There is necessarily a measure of confrontation. People sometimes think that you shouldn't be abrasive. But sometimes you have to be to make people acknowledge that they have done something wrong."

We all—each and every one of us—need to be part of these difficult conversations, these authentic moments of truth-seeking. Breaking out of our collective denial, courageously breaking our silences, and spending time listening must be the first step in a quest for a systemic, global effort for truth, restorative justice, and a better future.

The contributors in this collection, myself included, are searching to open up, to process our experiences, to break our silences, and to figure out how to describe the meaning and source of those silences. But this book is not for us. We share publicly, out loud, so that we may examine together why so many of us have been wandering alone, silently carrying our shame, our pain, and our fears; so that we may connect with and hear one another; so that we may heal together; so that sexual violence is no longer culturally-protected; so that we can live truthfully into our faith and trust in our shared humanity.

Flying Out Of Bed
Joan Kresich

SUSAN GRIFFIN, in her powerful book *A Chorus of Stones: The Private Life of War* said "I believe revelation is a human need, and even a property of matter."

But what if revelation is stuffed back down our throats, confined to the inside of our skins and held captive there? What if a tiny tentative foray into revelation is met with icy silence, or simply eyes gently turned away, signaling the end of dialogue's journey before it begins? What if all society's carefully crafted signals say, *Silence! Your story is not printable, not speakable, not worthy of the telling.* What then?

For decades I have held a story that way. A story that shaped my entire life, changed its course, like a mighty river changed by a dam. I know all lives are shaped moment to moment, by accepting one job instead of another, choosing this lover and not that one, by moving to a small coastal community across the country instead of staying put.

But for some of us there is another kind of moment that contains within it an alteration so nearly mythical that it won't be reconciled within a lifetime.

That moment for me was a night in the summer after high school, a night for which I have no memory. I drank too much, and a young man took advantage of that. I conceived a child. Because my mother was in the throes of schizophrenia and sliding toward her suicide, because of the great chasms created by family suffering, above all, because of the times, I was shuffled into a marriage with this young man. Huge steel gates slammed shut in front of the college where I was headed, and instead I slid down into a kind of underworld.

Just a few months before the #MeToo campaign lit up social media, I finally managed to write a poem, just one, about what happened. I doubt I'll ever write another. That poem was called "Flying Out of Bed". I did fly out of bed when my young husband kicked me in the back so hard I landed on the floor a few feet away. I had refused sex with him. I can remember other times of violence, but that one is indelible. I was about seven months pregnant. So many stress hormones poured into the tiny being waiting to be born, when he finally arrived in this world his entire body was tuned to the thrill-seeking highs of adrenaline.

Now there were two of us whose lives were altered. Now there were two of us who were poised to reap the harvest of violence. The seeds were sown; making repairs would be the work of a lifetime.

Of course I didn't know that then. Like all of us who find ourselves in trouble and alone, I hauled myself forward through what might be called will. And what exactly is will? I kept going. There was no support from my family; my parents were in their own blind alley of private suffering. When I revealed to my father (was my mother there? I don't remember) in the living room of our Berkeley home that my husband was hurting me, he turned me away: "Make a go of it." I must have walked out of the house understanding there would be no help, that whatever happened now would be up to me, but all I can see is the way he sat in his favorite stuffed blue chair, the one where he read the history of the civil war, the first world war, and the second, and the strange tone of his voice when he said the words 'Make a go of it', as though he were giving advice about sticking with an unpleasant job.

To leave the marriage (not 'my' marriage) brought the predictable onslaught; my husband became more violent. One time I called the police, but just like my father, he was not about to intervene. It was yet another humiliation in the daily string of them, because he blamed me for opening the door of my apartment to my abuser. When someone bangs on the door, you open it; how convenient for that policeman that the act of opening the door made me willing, so he would not be called upon to confront a male who used violence to assert his ownership of a female.

Willing and will. I was not willing. I was trying to use my will to become a captain of my own ship. But there was a fossilized code that had to be broken, a code of ownership of females, a code of males calling the shots, submerging the will of females when it conflicted with their urges and belief in their right to dominate. It was the twentieth century, but something very ancient was playing itself out in my one life. And in those years of searching for a way to break free, to break the code, to endure aloneness and terror of aloneness, I came to understand that ancient system, because it made its mark on me. That code burned my flesh like hot iron. Nightmares went on for decades, and the pervasive sense that I was going to be murdered trailed behind me and made simple tasks like returning to an empty house at night into something sinister requiring the need to check closets for an intruder who must be there.

I know why I haven't spoken about the violence that shaped my life. It was the perfectly crafted system of male dominance lashed firmly in place by all sorts of visible structures, educational, political and religious, by cultural expressions in books and movies, by cascading ads that smother our minds, by males with one part to play and females with another, all making speaking too dangerous. If the holding of pain is hard, the speaking of it to a world that does not want to hear is not a risk most of us will take. Yet there have been a few remarkably brave souls over these last decades who've told their stories anyway and kept the truth alive.

Every system of domination makes doubly sure its victims are seen as debased and diminished, even depraved. Slavery required slave owners to declare their human property less than human. Else, how could such an abomination be justified? Women victims of rape and male violence face all sorts of dehumanization. From the inside of this looking out, I think of us as messengers from the underworld, from a dark and dangerous territory, from a place no one goes willingly. Those of us who have been to that land have a message, which, as Susan Griffin expressed, needs to come into the light. It's not a beautiful story or an uplifting one. It's an ugly story. But it is that very ugliness that demands illumination.

Are we willing to hear the stories now? I'm not talking about the high profile ones, the ones that have the added valance of money and power and glamor. I'm talking about our stories, those of us who live commonplace lives out of the spotlight, cooking meals for loved ones, rising each morning and going to work, tending our gardens. Are our mothers, our best friends, the people in our book group or church community, ready to listen, to hear the extent of the damage? To search together for the portal where progress can squeeze through?

Since we're social beings, our actions have a ripple effect like a stone tossed on the mirrored surface of a pond. Punishing, retributive systems (and male dominance is in perfect lock step with retribution, depends on retribution) are happy to find someone to blame and dump the fury there. Restorative responses commit to a belief in co-responsibilities, which much more fully expresses our entwined nature as humans. Restorative systems use a wider lens, encompassing more of us looking at the part we might have played. That's what we need now. Who was silent in spite of suspecting violence was happening? Who neglected to actively teach their sons respect for women? Who failed to challenge a hiring system that favored men? Who allowed their police to carry on without a solid rape policy backed by training? Of course we need to hold men who rape and molest accountable, but we also need to understand if we don't commit to dismantling the entire system it will still be standing when individual men go down.

I have a relative who was gang raped just before her thirteenth birthday. Her mother never sought help for her; the moment she told her mother was the last moment her truth was spoken for decades. I think her mother was avoiding a potentially messy conflict with the parents of the neighborhood teenagers who raped her daughter. She played a role in the victimization of her daughter. My own father turned me away. I know he never raped or groped a woman, but he had a part to play in my victimization.

My father and my relative's mother could not have lived comfortably with their actions. (Before he died, my father, in a conversation about a topic unrelated to his failure to protect me, referred to himself as a 'coward'.) The protective impulse we feel toward our children is one of the most powerful forces we know. That the juggernaut of male dominance outweighed the desire of these two parents to protect their children only tells us how hard we'll have to work to dismantle and replace that system. But it also gives us the reason we have to do it. It's a system that hurts everyone.

If male dominance is an ancient fossilized lattice superimposed on every part of our lives, then the creation of the beauty we're striving for will take many forms. Some of that work will be the tender unraveling of a huge cultural tangle of threads so we can fully see the beginning strands of domination. We'll need to demand equal participation for women in every single public place where decisions are made. We'll need to look at our own part, as parents of both girls and boys, as friends and relatives of those who've been raped or molested, as co-workers of women who are being targeted, as citizens creating collective lives. We'll have to work close to home with ourselves and our loved ones, inside the gears of our communities where male dominance rages on, taking its toll every single day.

And revelation will play a part. Any of us can receive a revelation, and in those moments, become a part of the healing, a new place on our human map, marked by a gold circle. The beginning of a long journey. The place where the truth and a bright ray of sunlight finally come together.

Misogyny
Melissa Dickey

"BOYS ARE JUST BAD, but girls are little witches," my Aunt Ailie says to me in a conversation about parenting. It is just one of many moments when, in conversation with her whom I love, I am struck dumb.

So, she seems to say, we should assume ill-intention among females, but boys are simply mischievous. Could that possibly be true? That there is something inherently duplicitous about being female?

She lives on the beach in Mississippi, though she never quite goes to the beach. She raised two children, a boy and a girl. The girl committed suicide at age thirty-nine.

★

Growing up, the word 'woman' was like a bad word. No one wanted to be a woman. We wanted to be ladies. I'd hear 'woman' spoken in contexts like 'that woman' or 'not a very nice woman'. Sometimes I still hear it shouted, a man calling to his wife or mother: "Woman!" The women call themselves 'girls'.

Could I have felt good about becoming a woman, about growing into a word often uttered with such contempt?

★

I'm sorting through a box of things from my childhood that my mother found in an old desk. I open a cheap paperback diary with prompts I'd filled in at about ten years old. *Who are your best friends? Circle the words that best describe their personality and style.*

One page simply has blank lines to write on, and on that page I'd written, "Jerry Conrad told Kelli and I that Jacob told him that if we didn't stop staring at him, he was gonna rape us."

I remember: a moment during recess on the blacktop. Our excitement at his approach, the best friend of the boy we liked, met with this warning, this message. And the game my friend Kelli and I had played, of giving looks to boys we liked, was over.

★

Did I know what rape was? Did those sixth grade boys? I think we did, at least in a general, abstract way. The mechanics of sex and violation were blessedly obscure, mostly, to my fifth grade self, and yet I perceived the threat of the statement. I wrote it down in a crappy diary, brushed it off, and told no one.

★

My friend Ceci is like, "That guy's just like that." We're at a small house party in suburban Baton Rouge, and a guy I don't know keeps staring at my breasts, trying to touch them whenever I pass near. I am twenty years old and visiting; I know two people there. His eyes are lowered and steady, his hands reach out. Surrounded by his friends, he ignores all conversation in order to stare at my chest. As much as I try to avoid him, he keeps coming closer. And he succeeds in touching them, in touching me, as I frantically tell him to stop, and jump away, pleading for someone to do something.

The room – mostly guys, all white – seems surprised by my reaction. Someone does tell him, half-heartedly, to stop it. I end up hiding in a bedroom, begging Ceci to get her boyfriend to take us home. Through the door I hear the guy drawling: "Where'd your friend go, Ceci? She's tall and thick and voluptuous…"

★

A few days later, I'm speaking to a friend – an ex-boyfriend, and the first person I ever had sex with – about what happened. We're in a strip-mall Supercuts in uptown New Orleans, waiting for his hair cut, as I tell the story. He doesn't have much of a response, which irks me. I go on. At some point he says, "Why are you making such a big deal?" He shushes me; he looks around. Apparently, I'm being too loud.

I suppose, in that moment, I expect him to care. I expect some outrage on my behalf, some friendly concern, maybe even some male proprietorship. Perhaps what he feels instead is embarrassment, though he does not say this. Embarrassment for me? Of me? On behalf of his gender? Of what should be kept private?

★

At that same house party in suburban Baton Rouge, before I decide, out of fear, to camp out in the bedroom with the door closed, a young black woman walks into the all-white room with a friend of hers. I'm surprised. I've only been at the party for a short time, and yet I think surely this is a bad place for her. The party seems to be composed mainly of Louisiana good old boys. I don't speak to her, though, and I give her no warning. I overhear one guy saying he'd met and picked her up at the neighborhood pool. Later, I see the two girls running out. The guy who brought them is moving fast through the house, yelling, "Where's my nigger? Where's my nigger? Where'd my nigger go?"

Laughter.

★

I am well into adulthood when I encounter – when I really hear – the idea of speaking truth to power. As a middle-class white Southern girl, I did not speak truth to power. I shut up, I changed the subject, I was polite, I was silent, I avoided conflict, I avoided the unpleasant. All this, I was taught.

★

My friend's family owns the house that Jefferson Davis lived and died in, in the Garden District of New Orleans. One day, home from college, I visit my friend there, and he invites me to meet his aunt, asks her to tell me about the house. She recounts the history like a tour guide. She calls the Civil War 'the unpleasantness'.

★

How would it be different to not be polite? To ignore the rule of not causing a scene? To tell my aunt to shut the hell up when she says to my friends, at a party she's throwing – in fact it's my baby shower – that she really knows how to 'nigger it up'. I say nothing, only cringe.

Silence long-standing in so many moments like that.

★

What good is it, really, to chronicle my (our) complicity? To note. To notice. To bring to light.

★

Who am I supposed to be in that moment? I should have criticized my aunt – not really my aunt but my dad's cousin whom I call my aunt – at the party she threw for me. But how?

★

"i had no model," writes Lucille Clifton. "i made it up."

★

The morning after a drunken fight with my cousin, in which I'd explained both why blackface in a performance is offensive and why regularly commenting aloud on a woman's appearance is wrong, my brother chides me. "Sure, you can talk about that, but not when you're both three sheets to the wind!"

The problem with me is, unless I'm 'three sheets to the wind', I rarely have the courage.

★

I have to complicate my relationships; I have to have these hard conversations. Don't I? It's part of giving up the comfort of privilege. Or so I tell myself, knowing I know best, or at least better than some people. Not doubting what I know. Still, how to do this? It's the right thing to do. Right?

★

While skinny-dipping in the Mediterranean Ocean. After drinking too much wine one night with people I've just met. The sudden brush of a hand on, around, under my breast. It doesn't feel like a come on. It feels like he thinks: that's for me.

★

I'm home from grad school, having a heated discussion at dinner in New Orleans with my brother and his wife. I'm all excited and self-righteous, high on my newfound understanding of white privilege, explaining that what we need to do is point out racism or sexism when we see it and hear it, whenever that happens, even among our friends and family.

"See, that's where you don't know me that well," my brother says in a sting that effectively ends the conversation.

★

Can I blame him? He refuses to risk his most valued relationships to point out a flaw in someone's worldview. He chooses acceptance and belonging instead. Also oppression.

How to choose acceptance and love and, also, how to criticize lovingly. A belonging that's not at odds with critique.

★

At the end of our first year living at the fancy New England boarding school where my husband now teaches, we stay for the alumni reunion weekend that occurs at the start of every summer. Our 4-year-old son and 6-year-old daughter are playing on the quad outside our dorm apartment. A few young alumni are out there too—the 'five years', the youngest alumni invited to the reunion, the ones with the worst reputation, expected to be least respectful upon their first official return for this party weekend.

One young man calls our son over to give him some 'advice'. With his female friend sitting next to him, he says to our 4-year-old: "Girls love us. Girls are for fun. Girls forget."

★

"It's the definition of rape culture!" I say to my husband when he tells me what the kids heard. That guy didn't even know how well he knew it.

★

When I tell friends, teachers on campus, what that guy said to my kids, they're shocked. But why? Wasn't he just thinking exactly the way we expect him to think? Is it possible to prevent him from regurgitating misogyny without his even knowing it? How many institutions are failing us (and him)? And what options are available to the young woman who sat next to him, who didn't respond as he said it? Who knows if she noticed or was bothered. Who knows if she disagreed. Maybe her convictions, too, are bound by fear and shame. I don't pretend to know exactly what she could have done. But I mark it, I take note.

A Small Thing
Andrea Roach

I KNOW THAT TELLING WILL DESTROY US—even though my aunt Lisa's touching seems like a small thing stacked against my parents' tumultuous lives.

My parents met in a time when interracial relationships were barely considered legal. My 17-year-old Irish-Catholic mother kept her pregnancy hidden for months until her belly swelled beyond the camouflage of big shirts and bulky sweaters.

"You're gonna lose that baby if you keep running up and down the stairs like that," my grandmother said shortly before she offered my mother a new car to have her baby in secret. She stood over my mother with her big bosom, twists of cigarette smoke filling a large but stifling kitchen, and she explained the benefit of silence. She lied. She said that her husband, Bill – my mother's stepfather – wouldn't abide race mixing and that it would be better if no one knew.

Bill grew up down South. A small, ugly man—he loved eating pig's feet and waxed poetic about the black woman in his parents' employ who raised him. It was unlikely that Bill would have rejected the child of his favorite stepdaughter due to race mixing, but his silence on the matter turned fiction into truth.

"Let a nice colored family adopt it," my grandmother said, "it's what's best for the baby."

It was common knowledge in both families that my father was abusive, and even though my grandmother 'hated that little bastard' for what he did to her daughter, she wouldn't let my mother live at home with a black baby.

Left with the impossible task of choosing one loss over another: give up her baby discreetly or suffer her mother's repudiation, my mother married my father and his violence on April Fool's Day, the day after her eighteenth birthday, saving herself the threat of an unwed mothers' home and saving me from illegitimacy.

I MEET MY MATERNAL grandmother, Nanny, for the first time when I'm five years old. I sit at her long blonde wood table, swing my legs and drink tea with lots of sugar and just a drop of milk. I'm wearing a purple polyester dress with a white collar and four long banana curls. I sip the tea unaware that I wasn't allowed in this house until now or that this visit is nobody else's business. When my mother says later that I can't tell anyone about visiting Nanny, she leans in close and stares directly in my eyes so I know that she's serious. I nod my understanding, and we quietly continue our secret visits to Nanny's house.

I like Nanny and her husband Bill. I like her cats, Dippers and Mittens. I like drinking tea in the kitchen. I like seeing the house where my mother grew up. I like running up the staircase that leads to her old bedroom. I like that I can make my mother happy simply by keeping her secrets.

THE MOVEMENT OF MY AUNT LISA climbing into my bed the summer I turn nine is a familiar orchestration. She pulls back my blanket and slides herself behind me as gently as possible. Her weight causes the mattress to sink and the bed to creak. Her body becomes a half moon that cradles me or when we're back to back, a sturdy place for me to rest. She's been doing this for most of her sixteen years. Lisa lives with us off and on. Sometimes I think she's sent to protect my mother from my father, but I also get the sense that she feels more at home with us than at my paternal grandmother's house, which is rife with its own brand of violence.

Lisa is tall, thin, and pretty. She has a spray of freckles across her nose. Her uncombed hair stands straight up on her head, and her breath smells like milk. With a chest as flat as a boy's, you wouldn't think that she's much of a protector, but we all feel safer when she's around because my father won't put his hands on anyone but my mother. When Lisa stands between my parents, guarding my mother with her own tiny body, I think she is brave.

Lisa helps take care of my baby brother and me. She gives us baths and teaches me the latest dances. If she finds me sad and alone, she'll sing the one verse of the Kookaburra song she knows over and over until my mood lifts. She is the person I am closest to in the world besides my mother.

ON WEEKENDS, my parents surrender to their pain and tall bottles of booze, separately, and sometimes together. My father is tortured by his ideas of a father he never knew. More times than not, these booze-filled nights end with the police banging on our door as everyone else in my neighborhood sleeps.

I tell myself that if my parents stop drinking we'll all be happy, but they can't stop. Drinking helps them forget that they both have a parent who hates them—it helps them forget how and why they hate themselves.

I tell the police, when they ask about my parent's fighting, nothing at all. I have the right to remain silent.

MY AUNT LISA sucks on her two fingers when she sleeps.

WHEN THE NIGHT is at its darkest and my parents' tongues are numb with liquor, they talk with clenched fists, inaudible screams. Mostly it's my father who talks to my mother in the language of cuts and bruises, but sometimes, when he's gone or in jail and my mother has some kind of breakdown, she'll bring thunder down on me.

One night my mother instructs me not to tell the doctor in the emergency ward, who will repair the bloody gash on top of my head, that it was her fault.

"If you tell," she says in a panic while we wait for a taxi, "they'll take you away from me." I press a kitchen towel against my wound and nod my understanding.

Losing my mother is my biggest fear. She is the person with whom I share this strange life. The only one who really understands. I am that person for her. And even though I am nine and she is twenty-seven, we have the bond of soldiers who've served in a war that's at least as long as my life.

I know my mother doesn't mean to hit me with the heavy bunk bed ladder even as she throws it. I know that her sorry, soaked as it is with tears, is sincere. It's just bad luck that the metal hook on the ladder split open my head and even worse luck that we have no choice but to bring outsiders into our family business. My mother, who otherwise instills honesty and high moral values, says that matters of violence have to be handled privately. She understands that words can tear us apart. Being silent is easier than getting people to see past their preconceived notions about who she is: nigger lover; white trash. Outsiders don't understand why she drinks, just that she does. My brother and me are the only good things in her life, she says. She can't lose us after everything she's lost already.

Saying the wrong thing (the truth) to the wrong person (the police, a doctor, or my teacher) can send my father to jail or me and my brother to a foster home. Telling gets people in trouble.

At nine, I understand that there's power in knowing someone else's misdeeds but I don't feel powerful. Most times, I'm just scared that I'll be the one who lets something slip, that a moment of weakness will make me the cause of whatever reckoning is sure to follow.

When the doctor asks how I split my head open, I don't mention my mother or the ladder. I tell him that I ran into the corner of the television set which is only half a lie because I've done that twice chasing after my little brother and needed stitches both times.

Growing up in a family of violent heartbroken alcoholics, I've learned that keeping my mouth shut is the best way to settle a storm.

A FEW YEARS before Nanny dies, she'll finally tell my mother the truth about Bill. She'll say that he wanted my mother to stay home and have her baby; that he had offered to make her bedroom a nursery. Bill's long dead, and I am grown when Nanny admits to her lie. I imagine the weight of her silence and guilt dissolving with each word she speaks. When my mother realizes that maybe she didn't have to endure fifteen years of abuse, it opens all the wounds she'd spent her life tending. She wants to rip her insides out and hand them to her mother and say, "This is my hurt," but she doesn't know how, the years of silence between them is a barrier too difficult to cross, her voice, too difficult to find.

WHEN LISA SLIPS INTO MY BED the summer I turn nine, she rubs my back, something she hasn't done since I was a baby. Her hand moves slowly down my spine over my round bottom and across my bony legs. She whispers in my ear, "Andrea, are you awake?"

I stay quiet; pretend to sleep. Feigning sleep is the only way to get some reprieve from my family.

I feel her fingers slide along the seams of my cotton underpants, move upwards over the material to touch the soft skin around my 9-year-old vagina. She rubs. She pulls her fingers from between my thighs, up my backside, and glides them along the other cheek. From the right to the left, her fingers move. When she feels that it's safe, her fingers find their way beneath the seams. She tucks the material of my underpants between my cheeks and thrusts against what she thinks is my sleeping body. Her coarse pubic hairs scratch my bare bottom. I keep my eyes closed unsure why her touching no longer resembles the affectionate stroking that I've known.

THE SUMMER I TURN NINE, my mother hides Valium, small pastel blue and yellow tablets, in plastic sandwich bags loose and in amber colored bottles in the drop ceiling of our small bathroom. She drags a chair down the hall from the kitchen, stands her petite body on top while I hold it for sturdiness. She orders me not to tell anyone about the pills or where she's hidden them. I nod my understanding.

She tucks the pills there in the dark, bringing them out on occasion to count: "five, ten, fifteen, twenty." She makes little piles and adds them up like money.

One night after she swallows handfuls of her blue and yellow currency with gulps of Arrow's coffee-flavored brandy sombreros, she falls into my bed and tells me not to call the police. I'm afraid to disobey her, afraid what will happen if the police come. I sit in the dark room, cry, beg her not to leave me and keep watch over her. I shake her as she fades in and out of consciousness to make sure she's not dead. In the morning, I wake in a panic, press my ear against her chest until she draws a stuttering breath. I don't tell anyone because the last time she tried to kill herself by cutting her wrists with a razor, men in uniforms took her away on a stretcher and she was gone for a long time. My father's mother told me, as they wrapped my mother's wrists in gauze and rolled her out of the house and into the ambulance, "You have to be strong for your mother."

Being strong for my mother is to understand that any hurt or fear that I may feel is a pebble compared to the mountain of shit she's dealing with every day. I have to be there for her, to help her, not upset her. It means that anything that's not a broken jaw or getting dragged from your bed by your hair can be shouldered.

The mornings after my aunt touches me, I pretend that nothing happened. I'm good at hiding things now, even from myself. I also know that if I tell my mother, she will be enraged, try to kill Lisa, get arrested, and once again the possibility of being swallowed up by a foster care system, where certain other abuses await, looms for my brother and me. This I am sure. So I do my best not to cause trouble. I protect my family from outsiders and themselves.

Lisa's sexual assaults don't last long. When the summer ends, she goes back home to start school. It is the last time we share a bed as children.

TELLING COMES WITH CONSEQUENCES. I don't need a chaotic family to teach me that; I got educated about the power and consequences of telling in preschool.

In the social world of 5-year-olds there are generally aggressors, victims who 'tattle', victims who stay silent, and witnesses who may or may not speak up. Just like our adult world. For 5-year-olds, there are rules established by parents and teachers that are enforced in different ways within the group. Tattlers enforce the rules and gain power by reporting infractions. But since no one likes a *tattletale*, not even

parents, this behavior is discouraged quickly and even punished when discouraging doesn't work. The other children,
sick of getting in trouble, gang up on the tattler, call him a
liar, and leave him to die in social isolation until he learns to
stop 'tattling'. Which he usually does.

I was taught that to survive in this society, I must not
get anyone in trouble, make others uncomfortable, or force
anyone to deal with a truth they've chosen to forget, most
likely for their *own* survival. When you break the silence
that you agreed to for life, when you can no longer bear the
weight of your silence, when you say that you were abused,
you rarely get to tell just one person, particularly if you're
looking for some kind of accountability. You tell the world,
you invite the eyes, the feelings, the opinions and judgments
of people who weren't in the room, in the schoolyard, or
in your skin. No one wants more hurt. Silence feels like
protection until we're strong enough to speak, until we can
no longer stay silent.

WHEN MY MOTHER eventually stops protecting my
father at her expense, and testifies against him in court, I am
ten. He goes to jail for two years. "He would've killed me,
and my kids would lose their mother," she says, defending
her decision to tell. It doesn't matter that testifying may have
saved her life, she still feels she has to justify breaking the
pact of silence.

SILENCE BLEACHES MEMORY. When you don't talk
about a thing, it fades until it seems it never existed. I don't
think about Lisa's touching for years, but those nights she lay
with me in my twin bed change me. I lose ownership of my
body. Once stolen, it's easy for others to take it. Growing up,
I keep all the date rapes, workplace misconduct, and sexual
harassment I encounter to myself. It is my hurt to carry, my

problem to shoulder. I am *strong*. Self-preservation is all I know.

I'll talk about my aunt only when my uncle, Lisa's younger brother, kills his girlfriend, and reveals that my aunt molested him when we were children. I am twenty-nine. My uncle is thirty-one. We've been close our whole lives and neither of us talked to the other about Lisa.

I go to my grandmother's house when the allegations surface. My father's family gathers here almost daily to discuss my uncle's situation.

"He's lying," says one relative. "I don't believe it," says another.

I feel myself spin, all those years of rationalizing why I shouldn't tell is being challenged in the most urgent way.

"He's telling the truth," I finally blurt out, thinking that somehow this will help him. "She touched me too."

The syllables leap off my tongue, spring through the air, and assault the illusion my family has of itself. I watch it happen.

The room hushes, their thoughts grow loud. The small condo becomes a tense tribunal as each person lowers their head and considers my testimony. My father and another aunt squirm, avoiding my eye contact like they're trying to empty my words from their heads. "I can't believe it," each one says in a whisper. I wait for someone to ask me a question. *Am I okay? What happened? Will I tell my mother?*

They say nothing.

I Matter
Caroline Numuhire

I MATTER. This is a concept that took me nearly 30 years of my life to understand.

As so many young girls around the world, since my early days, I was wired to please: be a wise child at home, and your parents will be happy; be a smart student at school, and your teachers will praise you; and be a spiritual kid at church, and the priest will bless you.

Earlier this year, with two of my close friends, I started a 30-day self-care journey. We were tired of investing our emotions in boys who took our deep care and kindness for granted. What started as boy-healing exercise ended up being a truly transformative self-discovery process. The journey was made of seven steps and included daily exercises such as journaling, dancing to an empowering song, watching a motivational video, reading a self-love quote, or giving yourself a loving hug and positive talk.

In the course of the process, we fell into a form of detoxification. Unknowingly, we had accumulated incredible amounts of socially-inflicted and self-perpetuated pain since childhood. I discovered that I could not identify any moment in my past where I was kind to myself without feeling a sense of associated guilt. As this discovery emerged, my daily exercises included embracing sorrow and deep crying. I have, for too long, denied the humanity within me. I believe that God created the best in me so that the world may benefit, but I have not been including myself in the world that benefits within that belief. Instead, the core belief that women are meant only to serve has been stamped as an indelible tattoo on my feminine brain.

The unlearning process itself was as painful as the realization of the invisible box of societal expectations that trap and shrink women's wholeness. Despite our power to accomplish great things as human beings, we have not sustainably figured out how to teach each other the courage needed to believe in what our hearts know best. We are wonderful creatures, all of us: women and men. We matter, and yet are often taught otherwise.

I would be lying if I had to stand up and say that self-discovery is not terrifying, particularly to those of us who have been entangled in accepting pain as normal. But one of the most guaranteed fruits of the brave act of self-discovery that I can testify to is the development of self-worth—a simple belief in my endless value that allows me to sing with the morning birds that I do matter.

This song should have been my mother's anthem when she was pregnant with me, a melody to rejoice and recognize the uniqueness that I was adding to Mother Earth's heritage. We did not land here by chance. We all bring value to this planet. I wish someone had murmured in my ears growing up that I matter; that my childhood innocence ought to be preserved as a pure treasure; and that no man was ever allowed to displace his words or hands towards my precious body.

Instead, as I grew up, I had to learn that such intrusions on my body and my childhood innocence from men had a name: sexual violence.

Surprise. Surprise has always been my initial reaction when a man approaches or violates me in a way that dishonors my physical and spiritual being. The word 'unbelievable' flashes in my eyes, in effect paralyzing my muscles. In red letters, that one scary word, engraved to a visual backdrop, reminds me that this girl – me – is in the face of danger. And, in my case, the danger has a face, a human face, a male face.

The first time was during summer 1988. I was just ten years old, a bright kid that all teachers praised because I would shout out answers to their questions before they could finish framing them. It was the end of my P4 class, and I was visiting my godmother at Rwamagana, a city located in the Eastern Province of Rwanda. One afternoon, my godmother asked me to get ready as we were going to visit and assist a neighboring family. The man that we were visiting was a widower. A father, just like my dad. As we were standing in the circle, adults discussing and kids silently staring at them, the man jokingly said that he was looking for a replacement for his late wife—his late wife who had been buried earlier that very day. Even with my limited ten years of life experience, I did not find the joke funny at all. While he was still laughing, he reached out his hand to check if I was growing quickly enough to consider me an option. I was flabbergasted by his loud thoughts and that no adult slogged his hand or told him that his gesture was not only inappropriate to me but also disrespectful to his late companion.

Twenty years later, I cannot picture his face, but my body remembers the mark of vulgarity and disgust from that unwelcome touch. I was surprised that among those standing there laughing not one reacted when the widower continued, announcing after a clear analysis that I was still a child and further suggesting I should put an *inyagaruzi* (a small worm from the banks of rivers in Rwanda) on my chest to make it sprout quicker. That was it. Laughter. Silence.

No one predicted how that moment of humiliation would haunt the next two decades of my life, eroding on its way all the trust I had in men, in adults to protect me. It was just another unwritten and forgotten human story buried behind the guise of the conservative cultural norms of my beautiful motherland.

A cocktail of silence and anger followed my surprise as the adults around me transitioned from his words and gesture to the next subject of discussion: the CECAFA, a regional soccer competition that the Team Rwanda B ended up winning later on that year.

Reflecting back to that dry season of 1988, I have always wondered why I never shared the incident with my godmother as we were walking back to her house, hearing frenetic echoes of sports journalists who were commenting on the CECAFA Cup. I have wondered why I kept silence later that day when I was eating the delicious rice and fish sauce she had cooked for us. When I laid down on the bed that night, I asked God to forgive me because I had sinned. I fell asleep with a rosary wrapped in my young hand, convinced that God had not fully purified my body.

I blamed myself and did not dare to open up to my mother weeks later when I returned to Kigali where we resided. I did not know how to start the conversation with a mother who had warned us about purity; a mother, who since the beginning of our lives, told her daughters that she would kill herself if one of us ever get pregnant without a husband. I kept silent about that incident until today. In my silence, lives the feeling of that moment that I still carry with me, almost as a birthmark or a childhood mark, somehow a stain of dishonor.

Four years after that incident in Rwamagana, on January 2nd, I was home in Kigali while my family was still celebrating the New Year in my father's home village. I had stayed home because I had the second sitting of Geography, and

I had to retake the exam the following day. My dad was worried and thought that his little girl was not safe home alone with the houseboy. He urged a cousin to come and spend the night to keep me company. I was nervous preparing the exam because if I had failed it, I would have to retake the school year. It was during a period when Rwanda was experiencing serious blackouts, and I remember that there was no power during dinner that night.

After dinner, I cleared the table and put all the dirty dishes in the kitchen sink. As I was planning to wake up very early to review my notes, I did not see my cousin approaching me. Surprise. Again. My body was paralyzed just like four years prior in Rwamagana. Perhaps frozen this time in part because it was my cousin—the evil, who happened to be married, had a family face and name. What saved me from a certain rape was that my incorrigible cat, who in an attempt to steal a piece of meat from the food leftovers, broke one of my mum's floral porcelain plates. The clash of the dish on the cement ground surprised my cousin, and he instinctively released me. I ran to my room, locking the corridor and bedroom doors behind me. The next morning, I woke up as early as planned. One of the house's windows did not have any grilles but rather a metallic shutter. I escaped through that window and rushed to school.

Again, time passed. Silence. Every time that cousin would come to visit us – yes, he dared to come back – mum would ask one of my two sisters or me to prepare the guest bedroom for him. When it was my turn, I would beg my sisters to do it on my behalf. They would always refuse. Sometimes, mum would get upset that I disobeyed her orders. We all resisted completing those ordinary requests when he was around. It was later on, still in our adolescent lives, that my big sister asked why I resisted:

"He is weird!" I replied in Kinyarwanda.

"How weird?" She asked me.

"*Il a les mains baladeuses!*" I timidly responded in French. He has wandering hands.

Our collective silence broke in that moment. Both of my sisters had experienced similar kinds of violence from the same cousin. Luckily, by that time, we had read so many books from around the world, and we knew we had to talk to someone. Suddenly, we were all in it together, as sisters, as a collective voice. Sisterhood, what a united strength it gave us! We told an aunt whom we trusted. After talking to other cousins, she discovered a nearly identical story over and over again. Our aunt had a conversation with him. He apologized to all of us.

In the months that followed, our cousin came back home. When we saw him again, we could read deep shame on his face. His shame was not a satisfying consolation to us. What made us feel safe, however, was observing the new pattern of his behavior– he was no longer trying to touch our young bodies. That allowed us, very slowly, to sit in the same living room with him, even when our parents were absent. It took us time, time to watch, analyze and interpret if the predator in him would unexpectedly awake and hit. It has never happened again to us. Now, his old behavior has become a joke among the female members of my family.

Forgiveness is possible, although there is a portion of innocence that is lost forever when women and girls experience sexual violence. But what I call forgiveness is actually the act of letting go of things that hurt me and enjoying the gift of every day's joy and love. I wish my memory could erase these incidents so I can regain my full sense of safety, but it can't. Instead, I have slowly learned how to find beauty in the present moment without carrying all the luggage of yesterday.

A culture like mine, where talking about sex is still taboo, prevents girls from opening up about any case of assault. In my case, having an aunt who believed that I was telling the truth built so much confidence in me that I no longer tolerate any insane comments about my body, my clothing, or worse any misplaced gesture from anyone. It does not mean that incidents do not happen here and there. The difference between now and then is that today I have a voice because someone once believed my story such that now I can believe in myself, which is enough for me. I now stand, speak, and fight for myself because I know, intimately, that my safety matters in this life on earth.

My self-discovery journey taught me that I deserve respect for all aspects of my life from people—all people, myself included. I am not only a victim but also a fighter. Every time something happens, which is sadly too often, I try to confront the man, not in an aggressive or arrogant way, but with a gentle firmness, sharing the impact of his actions or words. So often, it is people who are part of my everyday life who perpetrate these types of violence. I have misinterpreted a man's intention in the past, and it was important for me and him to clarify things. I have learned that I cannot relocate all those who perpetrate such violence in words and actions outside of Kigali, so I talk to them because we still have to co-exist.

For me, the firm and polite confrontation has proven to be one way of preventing escalating forms of sexual violence. Silence is no longer an option for me and some men just need to be confidently told:

"You have to stop. I do not appreciate your behavior!"

Some will stop.

But more importantly, I have come to believe we have to empower men. Men have to stop being told and believing that they are sexually-driven beings who cannot control their primitive instincts. There are several role models for the widower and my cousin who abused me—the role models are men who have never abused women. So, socially and culturally, we need to stop shrinking men's potential—they are all fully able to behave as respectful beings. Sexual violence is not a natural male thing as sometimes we've been told.

Men have to be taught how to break their silences about sex, how to ask for permission from women, and how to keep checking in with their partners to be sure they are not abusing their power. I'm not sure how to do this. What I know is that keeping silent when we've been victimized is to allow self-suffering while granting our perpetrators the right to walk away. I have come to learn that I would have never gotten the inner courage to challenge people on sexual violence if it was not motivated by the desire to protect the fragile little girl who lives inside me and still needs protection. That same fragile little self exists in men too, and we can empower them by teaching them how to lean into the power of vulnerability, which is anything but weakness.

Healing Silence
Esther Diplock

WE OPEN WITH SILENCE, in a circle as strangers. I catch the wary gaze and feel the anxious shift of others in the quiet. I am co-facilitator of the space and I know, underneath this silence, within the individual's inner worlds, live untold stories of gender pain, sexual trauma, and violation. They have each arrived courageous and yet fearful as they anticipate exploring their own experiences in the forum of this Gender Equity and Reconciliation workshop.

On this first morning of the workshop, we sit together in a polite, slightly uncomfortable silence. I have sat in these circles many times, as both facilitator and participant. I know before our three days are finished I will hear – spoken into this circle – profound and painful stories of sexual assault and gender pain. Some of these stories will never have been voiced out loud before. Together we will defy the cultural norms of silence and speak our stories in this diverse group where we represent different genders, sexual orientations, cultures, and backgrounds. Founders of the work, Will Keepin and Cynthia Brix, speak to the essence of the work in their book, *Divine Duality: The Power of Reconciliation between Women and Men*, when they say: "women and men join together as equals, they get deeply honest with each other about their experiences, and through this process they heal past wounds, awaken to new realisations together, reach a place of reconciliation and forgiveness, and are thereby mutually transformed."

Before it is safe for these stories to emerge and transformation to unfurl, we will each face into our own resistances to speak out. At this point in the process, I often feel the residual power of my own childhood experience of silencing myself in fear of being abandoned, judged, and rejected by those I loved and depended on.

The profound paradox of this work is found in the way it melts the silences that harm by introducing a silence that invites and ushers in voice. The pressure of staying silent and being silenced has caused long-term, entrenched pain for many here. In this workshop, we invite participants into silence so that they may become silent witnesses to their own story and others'. This is the entry point into healing for individuals who need both to hear their own voices speak up and to be heard by people who will not be afraid of what they say.

I vividly remember when I spoke in my first circle. As I recall the moment, it is as if the years dissolve away, there I am sitting in the circle during what we call the Truth Forum—a time for stories to be voiced and for listeners to receive them in sacred silence. I remember my fear—it almost keeps me from speaking up. As we reach the end of the allocated time for sharing, I feel an urgency to speak my inner experience and yet a rolling dread of not knowing. Will I find coherent words? Will I allow myself to dip down into the flooding well of emotions inside me? Will I allow a tear or an angry voice to emerge? I know my voice will tremble. I will be breathless and quiet when I start. I'm scared I'll ramble through extraneous, unneedful, cluttered words, trying to find what I am so desperate to say. This old pattern of 'too many words' hides the words I'm not saying, allowing me to avoid my pain. I use words to keep me numb and undisclosed to myself. And I might use them to keep me hidden in this room full of compassionate and courageous individuals.

I am sitting in a tight circle with a dozen other women, chair to chair, almost touching legs and shoulders. Some in the circle are holding hands, others are crying. Many stories of gender pain have already been spoken. Outside the gathering of women, encircling us fully, sit the men. They have been invited into the intimacy of listening in sacred silence to the stories shared in the women's circle. I look around at the men listening. I see tears sliding down some cheeks; others hunched forward straining to hear every word. I feel a wave of compassion and care from these men who have already vulnerably invited me, a woman, into their own stories of trauma. I gain strength from looking at them. I have known other men like these in my life. Men with integrity who are willing to take responsibility for their share of silencing and their contributions to violence and abuse.

I feel shaky. My hands are trembling. It is the women I am scared of right now in this moment. I fear their condescension, their judgement. I believe they will belittle and dismiss the pain I feel. I expect competition and vying to prove their pain and their story is worse than mine. This fear has stopped me from speaking up so many times before. In the silence we hold together now, I remember what it costs me to push myself aside and pretend I don't have my own story. I was taught to neglect my own wellbeing and to emotionally prostitute myself, taking inappropriate responsibility for others' welfare. I deeply want to speak my truth to these women, and I deeply fear their judgement and rejection. I am here, surrounded by women and men, and yet feel so alone, so lonely.

The sexual violation I need to speak about occurred early for me and, in many ways, was more energetically and emotionally intrusive than physically. What was perhaps most damaging for me was a family environment that suppressed and denied sexuality. It was the silence of not telling my parents and the heavy shame of experiencing myself as sexually promiscuous, defiled, dirty, and dangerous in my sexual desire that was most damaging for my young girl self. In this family culture of not speaking, I learnt the toxic lesson 'Women are weak. Women are sexually dangerous'. It became the message I told myself: I am weak. I am powerless. I must do what others tell me to do. Never speak up. Hide behind a 'good girl' performance. Don't let others see who I am.

Living these beliefs trapped me. I grew up appearing well-socialised, outgoing, intelligent, caring, and a most spectacular 'good girl'. However this was accomplished at the expense of not speaking up and not expressing the fullness of myself. I kept forcibly hidden, behind layers of fat, the parts I demonised as 'bad girl'. I had very few female friends. I wanted older female mentors who stood in their own power and wholeness and who expressed themselves without shame. I longed for these women to show up in my life.

Here I am in circle with women who might be able to hear me. And when I finally open my mouth to speak, the story that emerges, with shuddering sobs and runny nose, is the gut wrenching grief of losing Widilia to cancer. She was the older female mentor and friend, who whilst struggling with her own guilt, shame, and silenced voice, had welcomed me into her life and embraced the parts of me others appeared scared and threatened by. She liked my power, my naughtiness, my wicked sense of humour, and my wildly open spiritual heart. I tell the story of losing her to death and gasp at the intensity of the pain I am able to feel here surrounded by other women, who lean in and hold my hand and cry tears with me. This is like cool balm and soft flowing water over my red raw heart. They are all silent. They listen to me and my story. It is my time to speak and my space to claim here in this Truth Forum. I sob again as I write these words to paper. I experience love and support and sisterhood. I allow healing and hope to grow in me. I am beginning to reshape old beliefs. I am beautiful. I am clean and pure. I am powerful. I speak my truth unashamed. I express myself and my sexuality with freedom and fullness.

It takes time and more circles before I speak up and own my own story of sexual violation. During the intervening time, I welcome and cultivate friendships with women I respect and love. And when the time comes, I do find words to speak about my sexual pain to the women and men I have chosen to invite into my life.

Now, having found authentic ways of expressing my own voice, I co-facilitate these circles, participating in creating the conditions that allows others to come out of their silences and speak.

Experience has taught me that silence comes in various forms and many emotions live within it. I have witnessed its presence when participants are restless and anxious, agitated about the unknown future. Silence often comes bringing fear, and for those who have lots that is unsaid and hidden, the silence often contains terror and harsh self-critique. I have felt the almost tangible silence that falls away when voicing of deep pain starts, then tears form in my eyes and my heart rate increases.

Conflict in beliefs and misunderstandings between participants at times lead to raised voices and strongly-worded disagreement. For those witnessing, a silence can occur where breath is held, adrenaline spikes and fear pushes in, as they wait anxiously for facilitator intervention. I have learnt in these times, to speak up and invite everyone to take a deep breath, to locate ourselves in the present moment, to pause, and integrate what is occurring within us and around us. This will often allow those who are in conflict to calm enough to speak their truth, without needing to force a change in the other. Here is where acceptance of difference can grow.

I have also sunk gratefully into the silence when at last the hush comes after truth has been voiced and a peace descends into the group. My favourite is the joyful silence of looking around a room and exchanging grins and meaningful looks with those whom I now experience new connection. Here my heart is wide open. I feel love for the group and I experience myself as 'one' with those around me. It is at these times I know deep healing is occurring and has occurred within individuals in the group.

I also know some in our circles may never taste and feel the full freedom of expression and healing of being loved and accepted as they are. Over time, in our collective stories of trauma, I repeatedly hear the theme of being silenced. Being silenced teaches the kind of silence that shuts down, closes off, and excludes; it is cold and harsh and full of fear; it tells us not to open our mouths and not to cry out for help. Many of us have learnt from being silenced to swallow our words and silence ourselves as we hyper-vigilantly scan the *other* sitting across from us, at home, or work or in a café. History has taught us that the one across from us is scared, preoccupied, dissociated, disinterested, aggressively angry or not able to cope with more than their own inner pain. For some, these lessons are so painful and have been repeated so often throughout life, they do not want to risk speaking up or they lose their words in the haze of terror at the possibility of being hurt again, rejected, abandoned, betrayed or ridiculed. I feel deep compassion and care for those living in the horror of this silent tyranny, as I have felt the sting of it in my own past.

I choose now to invest myself in this work, in the hope that some of those silenced will find ways to speak past their fear and taste the joy of expressing themselves freely. For this reason, the silence I seek to open in circle is warm, intentional, invitational, even whilst it is full of tumultuous feelings for those who are preparing to speak. I hold this silence lovingly and gently, as one who has listened, in the past, to my own stories and is now ready to hear others speak the truth of their own stories aloud. This is a compassionate silence, which creates a space for speaking; it contains hope for a future free for self-expression. It is a silence, which pauses to allow us to share our stories and move forward.

In her book, *Silence: The Mystery of Wholeness*, Cheryl Sanders-Sardello writes about the silence of entering the redwood forest. "To be here requires attention, listening, and gazing deeply without assaulting each thing seen with a conclusion. The silence here is not just in the 'what has been', it is most deliciously waiting, too, in the 'what will be'. Movement in the silence is towards, not away from." It is this kind of silence that we experience in the sacred moments of stillness occurring before and after a courageous voice speaks up in the circle and shares some significant part of their trauma story.

I love those moments, sitting in circle, when I experience us move towards each other as a group. For many of us, the change of breaking the shame-filled silence makes way to allow in a new silence of being peacefully present with ourselves and each other. I have heard group members share that, when this moment arrives in the workshop they feel a profound sense of connection, love, and belonging. Those previously isolated in the tyranny and loneliness of silence, have said they find themselves opening up, in a new way, and tasting what it is like to be peacefully surrounded by others, similar and different, who have listened and now welcome them into relationship.

As I reflect back on my journey of breaking the tyranny of my own silence, I know I am changed. I am increasingly free from being silenced by my own fear, others expectations or social pressure. I commit to speaking up in my daily life, and I experience growing freedom to express myself. I choose, more frequently and cleanly now, when and how I express myself. I have a growing capacity to quietly sit and listen to my own voice and others', and I am courageously willing to bring the person I am uniquely into the world and into relationship. As a result, I now have deeper, more intimate relationships in my life. And, yes, I still bite back and don't voice my opinions at times, especially when those I care about express their difference or offer me their disapproval. I still fear rejection and feel the pain of silencing parts of myself.

Even whilst I am in the difficult process of breaking the tyranny of silence in my own life, I notice a beautiful experience occurring. As I risk speaking up, I am able to accept myself more easily—I am falling in love with myself. And as I listen, in reverent and respectful silence, to others speaking their truth, I hear their hearts, I am more accepting of who they are, and I frequently find myself loving them. In voicing our stories collectively, a loving connection is created. In these circles, out of the silence, I have tasted a love greater than me, a Divine Love, a Universal Love, a love I don't have words for. In these circles, I dare to believe that love invites us to take a small and significant step towards transforming the shame, breaking the tyranny of silence, and beginning to heal our world together. We need such pockets of love and connection and healing in the midst of a world where sadly destructive silence is still a painful reality for many.

May we all continue to find and create safe silence, learn how to trust our own worth, open our hearts, and speak ourselves into healing and loving relationship with one another.

This Is Why
Chelsea MacMillan

THIS IS A STORY about speaking up. I'm still wondering if I should have.

It's about 9:15pm. I sit down, tired from a long day of work, on an orange seat facing the back of a half-empty, Brooklyn-bound B train. A man spread-eagles himself across two seats near me. I notice him look toward my crotch. I cross my legs, tuck in my earphones, and hope to ignore him for my 40-minute ride home.

Creepy guys are, of course, nothing new. I can't recall how or when I finally learned to sense their presence—the first time my arm hairs stood on end, the first time I felt unclean with a simple glance. Was it after an older boy molested 5-year-old me at a neighborhood party? Was it in eighth grade when my band teacher showered me with special attention and praise over all of my classmates? Was it in high school when I had to make up a test for an ever-leering biology teacher, and something in me knew I shouldn't be alone with him, so I brought a friend with me? I have never known when to say something.

At the next stop, a woman about my age, late-20s, with brown hair and a round face similar to my own gets in and sits at the back of the car. Creepy Guy, the other young woman, and I form a little triangle. Surreptitiously, I watch Creepy Guy get up, stand over there, stand over here, and sit down again. His dark, beady eyes glance at me and her from beneath a black cap. I feel frozen. Back and forth, he looks from me to her and back again. He pulls at his pants. I think, *maybe he's itchy.* He starts tapping his crotch. *Oh my God, I think, this is really happening.* This guy is masturbating on public transit. I've heard this story before, and now it's happening to me. *What the hell do I do?* I sense his gaze on me. I pretend not to notice. Unconsciously, I reach for my hat and shrink into my seat, trying to cover up though I'm wearing a puffy winter coat and half-hoping to disappear in the process.

Numerous and conflicting emotions swim through me all at once. I feel stupidly annoyed because I'd rather be reading a book, not being reminded of these things happening in the world. I feel pity for Creepy Guy and wonder if he was ever neglected or abused. I wonder if the early humans used to masturbate around each other and if it's simply our modern culture that has pathologized sexuality by relegating it to private spaces. I'm sad that he doesn't know the beauty of romantic intimacy; why else would he need to get his kicks on public transportation? I feel unsafe – violated – and that surprises me. There's nothing unusual about this story. This is just one more to add to my own list of creepy guys. Surprise turns to anger for all women who have to deal with this shit on a regular basis.

I watch the only other person in our area – a young-ish dude engrossed in his phone – move away when he realizes what Creepy Guy is doing. *Thanks a lot, Young Dude, for abandoning us.* I consider moving away, too, but I can't leave the other woman there alone, hemmed in by the masturbator. I feel protective of her and oddly bonded with her by this revolting act.

I decide that I, unlike the half-dozen women I know who never spoke out about the men they've witnessed masturbating on the train, will report this act of sexual misconduct. I take out my phone and sneak a few pictures of Creepy Guy. In one of them, he has his phone out, angled toward me. I have the feeling that he's secretly taking photos, too, and I am horrified at the thought of him having a picture of me. I almost laugh out loud at the sick irony of the two of us mutually taking pictures of each other.

He moves back to the door, taps himself some more. He sits down, and the next time I glance over, his penis is actually out of his pants. Oh dear lord, he's actually twirling his penis. Maybe I should yell at him to knock it off. But, this guy looks dangerous. I keep my mouth shut and pretend to read something on my phone.

Eventually, he gets off. The train, I mean. I watch him walk across the platform and board another train. He looks around. Is he searching for his next target?

When I get a bit of cell service, I type 'how to report sexual harassment nyc mta' into the search bar. Within seconds, I am hurriedly typing into little boxes on an online form. I take a moment to walk over to the other young woman to ask her if she saw anything that I should add to the submission. She looks surprised. "I didn't notice a thing!" I feel a sinking in my chest. I walk home alone, feeling jittery and unsure of myself.

Two nights later, I walk down the block from my house to meet Detective Chichotky, the NYPD officer assigned to my case, at the 71 precinct (pronounced 'seven-one'). On the way, I begin to doubt myself. *What will happen to the guy if we actually catch him? Would anyone ever help him with his obvious sickness?* Maybe I shouldn't go through with this. On the other hand, he seems dangerous. Masturbation is relatively harmless, I guess, but what could it lead to? What has it already led to? I decide that, even though I might not be making the 'right' decision, I am making the better one.

I spend about an hour inside of the Special Victims Unit with Detective Cheech, as he invites me to call him. I feel like I have walked onto the set of a cheesy '90s cop movie. A handful of men swagger about the shabby-looking office, lazily typing at Windows computers, laughing and teasing, debating about what to order for dinner. I wonder if they would act differently if I weren't there. They keep glancing at me and, from time to time, lower their voices as if to be respectful. A severe-looking woman, the only other female in the room, occasionally furrowing her brow at a document in her hand. A big flat screen plays ESPN in the background. On the far wall, I notice a dark, empty jail cell. I long for the comfort and safety of my home.

As I drink in every detail of a scene I've never imagined myself in, Detective Cheech asks me the same questions he asked over the phone yesterday. I can't tell if he's just forgetful, didn't take proper notes in the first place, or wants to make sure that I give consistent accounts. *What was the man's skin color? Age? Height? Weight? Facial hair, jewelry, tattoos?*

I have trouble paying attention to the Detective. I wonder how many women have sat before him in this dingy, uncomfortable office, detailing gruesome incidents of sexual assault and rape. I am grateful that I'm not telling one of those stories. And I can't help but wonder, how would this feel different if I were talking to a woman? Or if we were in a private office, maybe one with a window and some flowers in a vase?

Detective Cheech hands me a black binder labeled 'White' in neat handwriting. He tells me I can look at the photos on my phone to jog my memory, but after that, I am not allowed to compare them to the photos in the binder. I feel nervous. *What if I get this wrong? Does the Detective think I made this shit up? Am I just being dramatic?* I shove that thought aside and tell myself I am doing the right thing. I'm unconvinced, but I take a deep breath and start flipping through the 8.5 by 11" mugshots. I am more than a little surprised to see Creepy Guy after just a few. I mark the place with my hand and quickly make my way through the rest of the photos, but no one else looks remotely like him. Cheech asks if I'm sure that's the guy; he could show me more photos on the computer if I want. Driven more by curiosity than justice, I figure it can't hurt to look.

Detective Cheech sits me in front of his computer. I click the 'NEXT' button over two hundred times, looking at mugshots of men who've been arrested on the New York City subways for sexual misconduct: hundreds of men who fit specific demographic criteria of white, middle-aged, heavyset, between 5'6" and 5'10". Paunchy jowls, gaunt cheeks, hooked noses, bulbous noses, bald heads, ponytails, *peyos*, goatees, stubble, mustaches, ears that stick out. Blue eyes, brown eyes, beady eyes, round eyes, glassy eyes. Every pair of eyes seems angry, sad, confused.

My heart begins to feel heavy, and I feel sick to my stomach. All I can think is *how did they get here?* These are real people I'm looking at. They're husbands and fathers. They're executives and cooks and janitors and teachers. All of them are sons. All of them have committed 'public lewdness', in the words of the court. When's the last time any of them were hugged or touched with even a trace of sincere affection? When's the last time they expressed their own tender feelings to another person?

Toxic masculinity is an increasingly obvious problem in this country and around the world. Centuries-old cultural norms have pressured men to be strong to the point of aggression and self-reliant to the point of stifling any emotions deemed weak, vulnerable, or effeminate. Toxic masculinity is the glorification of guns and violence.

Toxic masculinity is sexual assault. Toxic masculinity touches all of our lives. The very justice system in which I sit is
dominated by men, almost all of whom play right into the
rigid gender norm of Tough Guy.

Not one image has come close to the likeness of the
perpetrator since the one I'd marked in the binder. I would
bet money on it being him. The Detective nods slowly but
says nothing. I can't decipher his reaction and his silence
makes me feel doubtful again. He fiddles around on the
computer. I stare at a fish tank, full of water, but strangely,
no fish. The other detectives decide on pizza.

Minutes pass. Cheech tells me we're all done. As I wrap
my scarf around my neck, he asks if I would be willing to
ride the subway with him to see if we can find the man. We
make a plan to meet, and he tells me that, in the meantime, if
I see Creepy Guy, to call 911. Okay, I say. I pause. Detective
Cheech, what will happen to the guy if you catch him? He
shrugs and says he'll be in jail for a while, get released, and
then eventually get thrown in again. "There's no rehab or...
anything?" I ask weakly, already knowing the answer.

Detective Cheech asks if I want a ride home. I politely
decline and walk the block-and-a-half in the cold sprinkling
rain, more aware than usual of what could be lurking in the
shadows.

A few weeks later, I receive a call from the Detective.
Could I come down to the station to identify him in a lineup? I make my way to the Lower East Side where they have
him. It's dark, and even though I'm ostensibly on my way to
make the city a safer place, I feel unsafe walking through this
empty, industrial area of town.

At the station – another sad-looking place – Cheech
ushers me to a tiny room littered with cigarette butts where
two women about my age are sitting in folding chairs.
Jeopardy plays on a TV screen on the wall. The Detective
tells the three of us that we are here for the same reason, but

that we are not allowed to talk about it. Of course, as soon as he leaves the room, we start sharing our experiences. I feel relief wash over me, knowing I'm not the only one to file a report. One woman, perky with blonde hair spilling from a messy bun, said she wasn't going to do anything until her boyfriend encouraged her to do so. She didn't think anything would come from it. None of us did. I wonder if any of us really do now, even as we sit, waiting to view a lineup.

Soon, Detective Cheech comes back for one woman and then another. Finally, he ushers me into a room no larger than a closet, where another officer waits, silent and stony-faced. The only light comes from the room on the other side of the two-way mirror through which I now look—straight into the eyes of Creepy Guy. Even though I know in my head that he can't see me, my body is unconvinced. My stomach clenches, and I take a deep breath in a vain attempt to calm myself. I am afraid he can hear me, so when I mumble his number in order to identify him, I am asked to repeat myself.

The cops nod to each other, show me to the door, and I am left again to trek the dark streets of NYC alone.

A few weeks later, I tell my story to an Assistant District Attorney who's been assigned to my case. I feel relieved to talk to a woman, not much older than I, and even though she's rushed for time, she tells me how sorry she is that I had to go through this. She's eager to take this case to trial before he reaches the limit of time that he can be held in jail—90 days. She tells me that I'm a great witness – articulate and observant – and I suddenly panic at the thought of this man knowing who I am. What if he tracks me down in vengeance? She assures me that this is highly unlikely, but it is his legal right to know who his accuser is. This is not comforting.

I am paired with another lawyer, but we never go to trial. Weeks go by with no news and, eventually, I stop receiving calls from the DA's office. I have to assume that Creepy Guy was released. Who knows where he is now? The odds of him receiving actual help are slim to none. They were always slim to none in a justice system that is punitive, unsympathetic, and bogged down in processes that have nothing to do with healing for victim or perpetrator.

I am left to find closure and comfort on my own. Maybe I should have tried to brush off this very common occurrence into the pile of countless creepy guys I've encountered in my life. The only validating voice in my head is a worried one: *what worse things could have happened?* Validation grows into vindication as the urge to protect other women rises like a fire in my belly. I. Am. Angry. I am angry for all of the times I, and so many others, have been silent.

I know I'm not alone in having maintained a certain vigilance around men and boys since I was a very little girl. The questions going on in my mind at any given time are so frequent, they're like white noise: *Is he just being friendly or is he hitting on me? Is he crazy? Are my keys accessible in case I need to protect myself?* I feel like I have tapped into a deep well of exhaustion I didn't even know existed. I am simply tired of dealing with this shit on my own and yet feel uncomfortably aware of this vain attempt to find healing through the NYC justice system.

At no point during this rigmarole have I truly felt I was doing a good thing by reporting him. At no point have I felt safer—in fact, quite the opposite. I am tired and overwhelmed by interviews and lineups and stressed-out lawyers. And, somehow, I am supposed to find comfort in the fact that I was 'one of the lucky ones'—by mere dint of not having been physically assaulted. I hear a mocking voice in my head, "At least you weren't raped, Chelsea." I feel like I shouldn't feel so bad. And then I think, *this is the moral standard to which we want to hold men accountable? This is the level of trauma that's acceptable for women to carry with us?*

It's no wonder that women don't report sexual harassment and assault more often than we do. There's no infrastructure of healing in a punitive system designed to keep a man from reconnecting to himself and to other human beings. There's no healing for female victims sitting in rooms of tough guys with guns. What good was it for this sick man to sit in a prison cell for three months? What good was it for me to speak out in a society that is not built to hold my voice or the voices of other women?

This is why we stay silent.

Now I Can Say
Pamela Bettencourt

"MY FATHER DIED," she said, and my life erupted. It was Saturday, April 5th, 2014. I was nearing the end of my grocery shopping. My carriage was full as I was approaching the cash register line. My body went numb when I heard those words. I gasped for air. I was flooded with emotions. My head was spinning. He was surrounded by family. His wife was there. Did he want me there? Were there tears in his eyes? Was I in his final thoughts? Was there a final confession as his life came to an end? He had told me he was sick a few weeks earlier. He didn't sound alarmed about his health. He just wanted to talk about *us*. "Are you alone?" he had asked.

I considered visiting him in the hospital. I could have gone, but I was terrified he would reveal *us* or his family would confront me about *us*—that they would finally ask me about *us*. No one had ever asked me before—he was the speaker for us. I wanted one final conversation with him. To hear what he had to say now. But he died. And he could no longer speak for *us*.

You would have thought I would feel relief. The groping, the obscene telephone calls and awkward holidays, the inexplicable packages, and wondering if I was being followed all over.

But I did not feel relief. I felt pure grief. What was I grieving? I wanted to cry. I wanted to scream. I wanted to run nowhere in particular. I was scared. I felt abandoned. I was afraid I wouldn't survive. My partner in this charade was now gone. I felt like the bad guy now. I was alone with us. I didn't know how to be in charge.

I left my carriage full of groceries and ran for the door. I got in my car and sobbed. When I had let enough emotion out, I called my husband and told him about my friend's father's death. I sat and cried some more. I couldn't move. After an hour's time passed my husband got worried and called me back. I was still sitting in the same parking spot. Eventually, I managed to drive home, groceries still at the store.

I wanted to be alone. I went to bed. I lay there numb. My husband canceled our dinner plans. He didn't want to leave me alone. The next day was more of the same. I stayed in bed all day, just trying to survive. Unable to concentrate and with little to no control over my emotions, I had to try to go on with my daily routines. I had no explainable reason for being so immobilized. What would I say? When I did get up and go to work, I totally lost control while talking with my co-worker. He asked me what was going on, and he convinced me to get help. It would be the first time I shared my full story with anyone.

The guilt and shame of never having shared this huge part of my life with my husband grew over time. My husband saw I was jumpy. He knew I screamed a lot. He knew I had nightmares. Many fears and phobias. Conversations we should have had, we never had. I hoped help would allow me to build up the strength to tell my husband about us.

The story began in the mid 1970's when I was thirteen years old. My upbringing was the perfect situation to fall prey to child sexual abuse.

My family was the typical old-fashioned Irish Catholic family. We lived in a rural middle class neighborhood: my parents, three girls, three boys, and a dog. I was the youngest. I had a twin sister who was three minutes older than me. Early on, my twin sister and I shared everything, including our friends. Our curfew was when the streetlights came on.

My parents – good honest hardworking people – were blind to the fact that not everyone else was as nice as them. My father, quiet but stern, took care of his business himself and didn't ask for help. At times, he worked three jobs at once. He quit school in the eighth grade to help support his family and later on got his General Educational Development certificate. He took nighttime automotive classes to learn how to fix his own cars. He built our family home. His favorite kind of banking was done in a strong box under his bed. He believed that a person's word, followed by a handshake, made a deal official.

My mother loved everybody and was a perfect example of what she preached: "You get more from sugar than you do vinegar." With her apron on, she did everything around the house and never complained. She had part-time jobs here and there, but while we were young, she focused on raising us kids. There was one television in the house, and the kids rarely chose the programs. We passed hand-me-downs throughout the family. Respect really wasn't optional in our house; it was expected. No talking back. No asking why. As kids, we did what we were told, or we risked getting punished.

Nightly before going to bed, my father would set up his morning. He would place his cereal bowl and spoon on the kitchen table at his seat. On work nights, he would add to the table his watch and pocket protector with his pen inside. He came home from work at five o'clock and supper would be ready. After supper, he would watch the six o'clock news; we kids had to stay quiet while it was on. We went to four o'clock Mass every Saturday night. My parents went grocery shopping together every Thursday. My father ushered at church bingo every Friday night and was a member of a men's cribbage league. My mother made spaghetti for supper every Wednesday night, beans and hot dogs every Saturday night, and a big family dinner every Sunday afternoon. She always had a pack of Wrigley's spearmint gum in her pocketbook and enjoyed the afternoon soap operas with a cup of hot Lipton tea. There was a routine.

Sex was never discussed. We rarely saw our parents be affectionate toward each other. The only sex talk I remember was awkward and basic at best. The three of us – my mother, twin sister, and I – were together in the front seat of my mother's car. My mother never made eye contact with us. I remember my fear of her asking us questions, and I would accidentally get myself in trouble for knowing more than I should. But she never did.

When I was thirteen, a few weeks into a new school year, I made a new friend. She lived in a nearby neighborhood. We quickly became inseparable. Her house was very different than mine. She had just one brother, her mom worked full-time, and her dad was always home. They had a swimming pool, and they got to do a lot of things that my family couldn't afford. I was quickly treated like a part of their family, included in all the family plans, going out to eat, vacations, attending cookouts and parties. My parents were unconcerned about the amount of time that I was spending at their house. They were happy for me.

I thought he – my friend's father – loved me. He sure acted like he loved me. As a 13-year-old girl, I loved to hear him tell me how pretty I was. His compliments made me feel good. I looked forward to being alone with him, at their house every day after school waiting for my friend's school to let out. And one day, as if in an instant, my trust of him turned to fear. The atmosphere was different that afternoon. His voice was different. He looked different. Panic attacked me as I walked by his chair. Scared. Terrified. Confused. He gave me plenty of compliments that day, but they didn't feel good like before. Humiliation overwhelmed me as I stood there, letting him see my body. I had to do it. He was an adult. He told me to. I was confused.

My mother had always told me to keep my body private—a message that despite her good intentions filled me with hesitation to tell her or anyone else what had happened. I didn't want to start any trouble. He told me that he would protect me. And, suddenly, I needed him to protect me. We had to keep what happened a secret. Everyone loved him, but nobody knew the man that I had just seen. What had I done to make him do this to me?

He said nobody would understand *us*. I believed him. My father would have killed him. I didn't want him in jail. Each day after that one, he took *us* a little further. Night after night, for ten years, it continued. He stole my childhood. He controlled my adolescence. My silence and his control over me prevented me from ever having a boyfriend or going on dates. I never went to dances or proms. I didn't go to college or get an apartment. For him, for this secret, I pretended I wasn't interested in any of that. At the time, I didn't know why my life became so different than my twin sister's and my friends' lives. Now I do.

Living my life around *us* was deadly. At twenty-three years old, I felt like my life wasn't worth living. Life became stagnant, and I felt worthless. I wasn't living. I was slowly dying. I had to do something. I was at a point where I felt like I had nothing else to lose. I decided then that if I was going to die, then I was going to die trying to live. I made the decision, but I needed to find a way to do it diplomatically. I still had to protect us and I didn't want to hurt him. I cared for him. I hated him. I trusted him. A trust started by ignorance, a trust that fell into love, and a trust continued on by fear. He did everything for me. He even took living my life away from me. He manipulated me, hurt me, controlled me, yet at times made me feel good. This man had everyone fooled. He had a secret side to him that he protected at all cost, and he dragged me into it. I was forced into living a life that was destroying me. But I never told anybody about *us*.

While I began to despise living, I didn't really want to be dead. I wanted my life to be dead. I had to believe that I deserved to have a life. He instilled into me the fear that he would destroy my life if I told anyone. So I had to do this alone. I rehearsed what to say. I met him in his car. I was terrified to enter my unknown but determined to end my misery. I had no back-up plan. It was me and him alone in his car. I felt ready but when the time came he got in my head. I began hearing the many phrases that kept me submissive for so long. I felt my strength begin to fade away.

His sarcastic comment is what saved me. I wasn't paying attention to anything except his voice. Both in my head and in that car. I always listened to him when he spoke no matter what else was happening around me. I was trained that way. He said to me, "Look, even they want to know the answer." I listened to what he was talking about. It was the radio that he had turned on to break the awkward silence. I tuned into the radio and heard the words for myself, the chorus of the song called "Should I Stay or Should I Go?". It was perfect timing for what I needed to hear. I was a sign reader, and this was definitely a sign. A gift from God. I was rescued; my faith in myself was restored. I felt a gentle push to finally answer him, and I said it. "I want to go."

I met my future husband a month later. Another gift from God, the timing couldn't have been better. I was still trying to find my way into a new life. I had my freedom but not my confidence. I was scared and proud at the same time. People were noticing how happy I was. I wanted to tell my friend's father why I was happy before he approached me. I told him I needed to talk to him. He suggested the motel, I agreed. I never imagined the night would turn into such a disaster. I was there to tell him I had a boyfriend. Something he always said he wished for me. I felt for the first time that I was in control of the night. He wasn't happy. He lost his mind. He forced himself on me before I could leave. His fear written all over his face as he let go of me. He didn't say a word. I don't know if he feared what he had just done or the potential that I would confide in my boyfriend. I was still unable to speak of us. He eventually realized this and worked his way into my new life.

Our families were friends. I just wanted to keep the peace. My husband grew to know him as just a good family friend. He became like an uncle to my three children. The longer I stayed silent, the more I worried that speaking would ruin the life I had worked so hard to build for myself. I wanted my husband to understand me, but the risk of losing him felt too great. I worried that he wouldn't be able to forgive me for the years – more than twenty-five years – of not saying anything. I worried that he would feel burdened with my secret. I worried I wouldn't be able to trust his judgment if he wanted to speak with somebody about me if he needed support.

As my children grew up, keeping this secret became harder for me. My sons had intimate relationships develop, and I questioned my ability to guide them because of my experiences. I did my best to not smother my daughter. My thoughts about sharing my secret with them seriously changed when one day my son looked me in the face and said, "You will never understand. You have never had a toxic relationship in your life." That was agonizing for me. I couldn't speak freely from my experience in his time of need. This secret paralyzed me. And that day, I realized that the secret, my silence, was no longer just my problem; it was my family's problem. A revelation, I hadn't seen it that way before.

With a lot of help, I eventually found the courage to tell my husband. All my fears and anxiety over his reaction were laid to rest. He was shocked, sad, and angry. He felt betrayed but not by me. I knew I needed to tell my children to continue my healing. Two years later, after being admitted to the hospital for stress-related complications, I could wait no longer. The secret of my abuse was growing into something more detrimental to me than the actual abuse. The time had come to be honest with myself and my family about what truly happened. I told them. It was extremely painful for me to undo the image of me that I had devoted my life to creating. They had justifiable questions. They were saddened but I feel a stronger connection to each of them today.

This unexceptional image I created for myself must have contributed to the longevity of my abuse. My parents never suspected a thing. People in his life were concerned about his relationship with me. They spoke to his wife about us. She spoke to him about their observations. My best friend told her mother that she thought I had a crush on her father. She spoke to him about that, not me. Nobody asked me anything about our relationship. In my recovery, I have found this to be a common scenario. People go to the perpetrator with their suspicions—and because he is typically charming, manipulative, and convincing, the conversation generally ends there. And the person that suspects the inappropriate behavior dismisses their worries for fear of being wrong.

Since then, I have been learning how to speak up for myself. Time won't heal this wound—only I can heal it.

Holding onto my secret for so long left him in charge of my voice, even after his death. Letting go of my secret is slowly giving me back control. Being free to speak has given me the ability to heal. I deal with repercussions from those forty years daily, but the difference now is that I don't have to experience them alone.

Why We Are Hush
Patrick McFarlane

"We teach people what they are."

–Pablo Casals

THE FIRST TIME I was exposed to sexual violence, I was about seven years old, and heard my father beating and raping my mother in their room. I could hear her pleas for him to stop and then witnessed her naked escape from their bedroom, and concomitantly his drunken and unco-ordinated pursuit. While of course it was terrifying, the reaction in my body was to freeze and not move, to avoid drawing attention. I felt sawed in half by another desire to run and fell asleep hours later when the adrenaline ebbed and the pineal gland excreted enough compensatory melatonin. The next day, I woke up with excruciating abdominal pain, hoping that my mom would stay home with me. Not only did she make me go to school, but she also went to work. When I said we should leave him, she told me that I mustn't talk about things I didn't understand and that I hadn't seen her naked in the hallway last night.

We joke, now that my mom is 86 and I am 51, that everything was okay in our house as long as only we heard what was going on and the curtains were pulled so that no one could see in. When I called her to read this introduction and get her consent to write about this, she said, "I guess it's okay. It's okay. That was so long ago, I'm surprised you remember. I don't think about those things, they are just things that happen. It [this story] doesn't have my name right? I guess they'll have your name, but it would be hard to figure out my name now, and there aren't many people left from that time. It's just embarrassing."

And there it is... the embarrassment and shame that she still carries. I spoke with her for some time and again tried to squarely place the responsibility for such behavior where it belongs: on the perpetrator. We discussed the culture and system of laws. At that time, the police would come and 'talk with him' when he was drunk, giving him the proverbial walk around the block to sober him up, talk some sense into him. After all, it wasn't until 1993 that it became illegal in all 50 states for a man to rape his wife.

The boundaries of the law and the sanctity of the home sometimes mean tyranny to family dependents like me and my mom. Just like we have discovered in the hush of religious institutions, corporations, and political operations—family hush is encouraged by the same cultural and systemic collusion with violence. Speaking out – breaching these boundaries – pricks the notion that things are just fine as they are and makes society quake. And yet according to the United States Centers for Disease control, close to one in three girls and one in seven boys is molested by the age of eighteen in the United States. Things are not fine.

I HAVE COME TO BELIEVE that we are hush about sexual violence because we are hush, generally, about sexual behavior—and about the hopefulness and repair of intimacy. We make sexual violence something external, outside of us, outside our families because we have been taught to obfuscate, to close the curtains, to maintain a lie about who it is that is sexually abusive, and deny the potential joys of sex that remind us what it is to be connected intimately. It is useful to men – white men – to make this hush.

David Brooks, writing in *The New York Times*, identified in a survey why it is that so many people vote against their self interest in elections. He found that fundamentally it was an American delusion—that while tax cuts wouldn't be of benefit to the poor conservative voter, they reported that someday those tax cuts would be a benefit to them if they worked hard enough. A similar kind of delusion about sexual abuse seems to operate—if you ask most people to visualize a person with sexual behavior problems or a sexual abuser, they conjure up someone who is ugly, violent, distant, maybe masked, and a stranger, but more than 96 percent of sexual violence is perpetrated by someone well-known to the survivor.

We seem to struggle with holding the two disparate ideas at once in our minds that people are both healed and harmed in their families. The person most likely to kill you is your spouse. The person most likely to be sexually abusive to you is in your family. We don't talk about sexual abuse perhaps because it is painful to consider how it is happening all around us. Certainly we don't talk rationally about who perpetrators are because our own ability to be abusive is absolutely too painful to consider.

I BEGAN MY CAREER as a psychologist and social worker in 1996. Every one of my first ten patients, who were far more my teachers than I was their psychotherapist, reported a history of sexual abuse. I remember being stunned at the pervasiveness of sexual abuse and the minimal exposure to this knowledge that I'd had in graduate school. Quite quickly, I began to contend that the neat and tidy diagnostic criteria I'd been taught to follow were complicated by the fact that they don't seem to account for such violence.

One of my favorite social work professors at the University of Michigan, William Birdsall, used to quip that "social workers were the ambulance drivers of capitalism", meaning that sometimes social workers work at the edges of society to make things *just good enough* to avoid the need for any real system change, any revolution writ small.

Violence and sexual abuse are not only issues to talk about and explore from a distance in therapy—they are the result of constructed parts of our society where certain people are marginalized and at times rendered powerless by abuse. These parts of our society teach people who they are by defining their positions and roles in families, communities, churches, temples, corporations, and society at large. My father didn't batter my mother because of his individual experience alone, he did it because he could. Because he was taught that as a man he could behave in this one way with impunity. And my mother was taught to close the curtains and stay hush.

IN 1986, two researchers, Vincent Felitti and Robert Anda, found that sexual abuse − along with nine other adverse childhood experiences − is highly correlated with obesity, addiction, heart disease, diabetes, and cancer. It turns out that, on average, those of us with more significant childhood traumas die much earlier than those with none or fewer. And it also turns out that if we intervene, there is good evidence that resilience can be strengthened and we can prevent a host of awful things from happening to people.

While the work of Felitti and Anda is over three decades old, it still isn't part of a standardized assessment. In fact, the medical community has been largely silent in response to their findings. No real attention is paid to the research, and yet the ten adverse childhood experiences they measured can predict not only medical conditions that are likely to arise but also future experiences of violence, including future vulnerability to rape and domestic violence. In other words, understanding someone's experience of violence as a child can inform a public health approach to reducing risk of sexual violence among other things. And yet to do this, we must humanize medical interviews by asking direct questions and addressing the experiences people share so that they feel they can recover, they are not alone, and there is no shame in what they've gone through.

MARK WAS 23 when I first met him. He had come from a prison program for sexual offenders and had done a really good job of understanding his experiences both as a survivor and perpetrator of sexual abuse. Once he was comfortable in our treatment group, I'll never forget the vehemence with which he explained, "No one, until I went to prison, told me what normal was." He'd grown up on a family farm, where several generations lived in various houses and trailer houses on the land. His grandfather, as he described it, molested everyone. His grandfather would have sex with his mother in front of the kids, with kids, and with friends who visited. This was his experience from an early age. He described that when he was about 14, he sexually touched one of his sister's friends who visited the farm, and this friend told someone at her school.

Mark described, "The school counselor took me to the office, and asked me why I'd do such a thing that was so wrong, and then had a cop ask me the same thing. I had no idea what they were talking about, because no one ever used the words I was used to hearing, and when the cop asked me if I touched the girl, I said yes, and they got upset. But no one asked me how I learned that, or anything that got at what was happening. One cop told me I was sick, and I had no idea what that meant. It wasn't until I was 18, graduating from high school, when it happened again and both my grandfather and I got arrested, and in prison I realized that all families weren't like mine." He described in some detail his struggle to have reference points that were 'normal' in his quest to have a healthy relationship now that he had begun to understand what that meant.

Mark's case reveals what some psychologists have called 'guessing at what normal is', and I believe his story makes plain the case for the role of education and the role of asking direct questions in a society where sexual abuse is so sadly normal. Being curious can sometimes make a huge difference, opening the proverbial curtains and allowing for intervention to occur.

LILY IS THE PERSON who has taught me the most about why sexual abuse can be so confounding in development. When Lily was about nine years old, her father would hold her on his lap while he watched pornography and he would masturbate against her body. In her mind, when she told her mother, she caused her father to go to jail and her parent's divorce. I met Lily when she was 14 years old and a highly sexualized teenager, vulnerable to adults around her, and having sexual behavior problems with her peers. She had begun to expose herself and sexually touch her peers on her middle school playground and on the school bus, for example.

After some time, she explained to me that for her sexual abuse was confusing. Everyone had told her it was wrong, but from her perspective there never had been any ostensible violence, no experience of physical pain, and she had in fact felt close to her father in those times and wished they never had to end. She explained that she felt powerful in seduction and wanted to feel physical affection.

To this day when I share what Lily taught me about the confusion of some child sexual abuse with good physical feelings and affection, it can provide relief to patients who, caught in the boundarylessness of sexual abuse, harbor mixed feelings and questions about their experiences and about reporting them. Furthermore, Lily's sense of guilt about her family breaking up reminded me how seriously a victim often has to weigh the risks and benefits of reporting. My mom weighed the same such risks.

IN THE WEEK AFTER I heard my dad raping my mom and witnessed the aftermath, I remember feeling numb and baffled by the notion that going home felt exhausting. I wasn't sure that my mom could or would protect me or my sister from my father, and none of us could predict when his next drunk might happen and when he would be dis-inhibited enough to be dangerous. I needed a way to get through my school days at age seven and eight. Luckily for me, I had the experience of watching *Star Trek*, where they tackled the problems of human beings exploring the fringes of space, and my school had a great air exchange ventilation system that seemed to hum like the background noise that represented space in the television program. When I went to school, I pretended that I was traveling through space and thus had enough distance from my worry that I could do my work. My mom, knowing my interest, even bought me some shirts with Star Trek insignias. I found solace in this pretending.

Much later in my education, I learned about ego defenses like denial and sublimation and I could respect my mother's need to preserve 'normal' in a situation that was anything but. My experience in pretending helped me understand why and how we avoid talking about violence, sexual abuse specifically—it's to find solace, and to survive.

I find a kind of poetry in the telling of my own story and these clinical stories I am privileged to know—a poetry of survival and resistance. The power of these experiences is that they work against the catastrophe of the status quo, they empower us to open the curtains, to shed light on our delusions, and perhaps to drive change.

As an adult survivor of violence, I am in fact motivated to use my experience to teach doctors about interpersonal violence and how to intervene. The research is clear: not addressing trauma increases the likelihood that violence will be passed on to the next generation. The intervention needed is simple: it's to ask. Not asking, therefore, becomes a dereliction and a malpractice of sorts.

IN MEDICINE, the time is right to be interested in talking about sexual behavior, sexual abuse, and violence—to ask broad and specific questions with a curiosity and care that preserves dignity and highlights survivorship. By not asking the questions, we cede too much power to abusers, and we become complicit with the violence. No one who has experienced violence and sexual abuse should ever have to say, "No one asked me..."

But we struggle to address sexual abuse because we struggle with addressing sexual behavior. It is in teaching about boundaries, consent, healthy behavior, and sex that we can then make room to also talk about the reality of sexual abuse and how to address it. We need to talk about our bodies, attraction, connection, intimacy, and orientation—conversations that strike me as infinitely better than leaving our children disoriented in a violent world. It was President Bill Clinton (of all people) who fired one of the most remarkable surgeon generals, Dr. Joycelin Elders, after she suggested that we teach healthy sexual behavior, including masturbation, to adolescents. But I have high hopes that the public discourse resulting from #MeToo can help us deconstruct the ways that violence and sexual abuse have become accepted parts of our society and the ways that our bodies, attraction, connection, intimacy, and orientation have been hushed.

I have longed to open the curtains of my childhood home, and with this essay, my mother consented to let me. I told her, when I read this to her, that I considered her to be an amazing survivor of so many things. She said, "I never thought of myself that way, but I guess that is true." It's time to have this conversation about sexual abuse and to show another way is possible. It's time to find the beauty in the world, in ourselves, and in our most intimate relationships. This, my mom and I believe, is indeed a revolution.

Things Fall Apart
Monique Harris

"If you are silent about your pain, they'll kill you
and say you enjoyed it."

—Zora Neale Hurston

SILENCING PAIN IS LIKE putting a broken glass back together: the glass may be intact, but it will never function again as it should. The integrity of the thing it was is lost. One cannot trust it to hold what it could hold before. It won't even look the same. Webs of cracks will forever deface its form no matter how well it is put back together. Silence is the glue. And after a while, it will begin to dry up, chip off, and loosen. Its ability to hold the brokenness together will eventually give way. Things will not fall apart all at once. First, the cracks, then the holes, then a piece here, a slab there. Slowly, surely, and with time, things will fall apart.

When I finally told my mother about the sexual abuse that I experienced from her live-in partner, I quickly learned that telling the truth about being sexually violated was like taking a sledgehammer to a glass. My story was going to fuck it up for everybody. What I had finally had the courage to say turned out to be the crime, not what happened to me.

That night I told my mother, I learned that her perceived sense of status and security was more important than my safety. I learned that my mother was no longer my protector; she was just another adult in my life who betrayed me. She stopped the sledgehammer when I was in full swing, and the glass she'd glued together so carefully stayed intact. There would be no pieces to pick up that night; no shards to try to piece back together; I inherited her silence. We would go on as if I'd said nothing at all.

To speak of what happened to me was me wanting things to fall apart, which would be selfish, right? It would be my fault if everyone learned that my mother had let a predator into our home. It would be my fault that she would be single and alone, again. It would be my fault our lifestyle would have to change. It would be my fault if things fell apart. An already-shaky picture of domestic perfection was now a house of cards.

My mother was successful at keeping the outside glass intact, but what didn't shatter outwardly, shattered inwardly, and I have been dealing with the aftermath ever since. There was never any acknowledgment that I had been harmed or any thought that I may have needed help or support. I was never even asked what happened or about the extent of my abuse. Looking back on it today, I'm not sure how I coped with what I now understand was not just sexual abuse but also psychological abuse and parental neglect. I'm not sure how I managed to grow into a reasonably-sane woman considering the undiagnosed anxiety and depression that I experienced throughout my adolescence and into adulthood. I'm not clear how I managed to live in utter dysfunction without self-medicating with drugs or alcohol or how I managed to repress the pain and rage without harming myself.

The funny thing about silence is that the same silence can be different things to different people all at the same time. In my family, silence was protection for a pedophile, it was denial for my mother, and for me, it became a tool for survival. I had to learn quickly how to fend for myself and protect myself as I was forced to live with a sexual predator. I had to grow into adolescence without the guidance and wisdom of a mother. I intuitively knew and felt that the life that I was living was a kind of bizarre performance and that I'd better learn how to play my part.

So I did—I learned my role. In exchange for food, shelter, clothing, and the appearance of a normal life, I shut my mouth. My outside world would stay intact while I feverishly tried to make sense of what happened to me internally. I shut my mouth so I could at least pretend to have a mother. Life went on. I grew up, and no one was the wiser. I played my role well.

But I deserved better.

My safety, well-being, and personhood should have been my mother's first priority. But keeping the secret was her priority, and unfortunately, it still is. To this day, we have not discussed my abuse. Had my abuser not left her years ago, I suspect that she would still be in a relationship with him. I have accepted her silence. At the moment she silenced me, I experienced the severing of the attachment to my mother. The superficial façade of a relationship remained intact, while I navigated piecing together the shards of my psyche. It was a lonely, directionless road that I had to travel. There was no one to help me process all of the dysfunction that was my daily existence, no safe space, no respite. Trying not to reflect outwardly the damage that was inwardly wreaking havoc. Just trying to be a normal teenager, young adult, partner, mother-woman. Never feeling comfortable in my skin, never feeling grounded in my body, never feeling worthy of love, security or protection. I took the world upon my shoulders because trusting or depending on anyone outside myself was the surest route to disappointment. I am still angry at my mother. I barely speak to her, though I am not totally estranged from her. I choose in this season of my life to stop pretending – at least as much as possible – that everything is okay. She chose herself all those years ago. I now choose me.

As I've grown older, so has the glue that held the broken pieces together. As bits of that internal shattering come undone, I am more prone to sit and examine the pieces of me. Working with the jagged edges, the irregularities, the sharpness has all become part of my process of healing and true acceptance. And as the glue comes undone, so does the silence.

I may never have the acknowledgment of my abuse from the one who abused me or the one who made herself complicit, but I do not have to remain silent.

Somewhere, among the ruins of my inner landscape, were also the raw materials to create a life for myself that astounds me.

Silence is violence. The violent act of denying my story, pretending it did not happen, and never speaking of it again was more violent to me than any physical blows could be. How could I defend myself from the silence? How does one fight silence without power? I have overcome what has defeated others who have endured silence as a matter of surviving the unthinkable.

This is not an easy story to tell. This version is just one facet of a complicated journey that I am still navigating. I do not jump at the chance to proclaim 'me too' even with the multitudes stepping out of the shadows. I struggled with sharing my story not because of shame, but because this story is ever-present in my consciousness. This is not an experience that can ever be shared in its totality—only fragments can be shown. The labor of sifting through it all is more than enough of a reason to keep it to myself. As a survivor, sharing my story is my choice. At this moment in time, however, I also have the chance to share a very specific piece of my story that speaks to the oppression that so many of us experience in being forced into silence as others seek to protect themselves and abusers. For that reason alone, I share my story.

It is still difficult for me to understand the 'why and how' of this tragedy. It is still difficult for me to forgive, and I struggle with whether I ever will. There are those who say that one cannot heal without forgiveness. I do not know if that is true or not. I have seen many express forgiveness and still find themselves locked in cycles of pain and trauma. I am not as concerned with forgiving as I am with accepting that I have my own process of healing to contend with. That process alone is enough for me to work through without centering other people who have yet to do their work, who have yet to even offer acknowledgment that harm was done. Society expects that we forgive others regardless of how deep the injury, which I feel derails recovery and deepens guilt and shame for survivors. I prefer the term 'release' to describe my process. Releasing myself from the abuser, those complicit with him, and the pressure to reconcile with my mother gives me space to center myself in my story and to focus on my wholeness and wellbeing. Releasing has taken away the emotionally charged, misused, and often misunderstood notion of forgiveness and given me permission to piece myself together outside of the gaze of others. Maybe forgiveness comes after this?

Nevertheless, I remind myself that I was burdened with the weight of a story I should never have had to carry, most certainly not alone. Throughout my life, I have carried my story, managed it and even shifted it. I have pulled it, pushed it, held it, stumbled with it, but I have never had the luxury of putting it down. I have grown into a woman who has somehow held that story and found ways to turn the pain into purpose. The burden is still there, but the weight lessens as I understand that what happened to me was not my fault. It is my story, but I do not have to hold it all together anymore, I can let the pieces fall where they may, and I can admire my beauty in the brokenness that I somehow survived.

Exchange
Jennifer Jean

I can't believe these people,
says 'Flannery',

They're building these casinos
so close to homes. Pimps make you
work
those hotels forever.

Everyone in Starbucks
can hear
our exchange

over the blender & bustle. So,
I turn off
the recorder. Stop interviewing. But 'Flannery'
keeps

musing,

People notice nothing. *I got beat*
in one suite & thought for sure—
someone knows

Jennifer Jean

& hears me bloody
murder screaming.

But – no –

I nod, *Yeah…*
people. & I see her

bruise up
when, really, she matches her flan frappuccino—
all okay, all foamy
& tawny-schemed
in drifting layers. We sip our sweet
refreshments,
stare off.

★

She says,
A reporter once paid me to talk
about 'the life'. I open the door
& he gets up, off the bed!
We got, like, 5 minutes.

I nod & turn & see
this retiree,
in racing shorts & pulled up tube socks.
He's totally listening.
He hasn't unstiffened

in his fireside armchair
in forever.

★

Exchange

I wonder if I can find him, she says,
Pay him
to write a story. To get the word out. I remember
he called me 'Sunny'.

I say, *The paper pays him.*
&, I think about the two of us
working the power

of words. How, soon, I'll be
poeming. How 'Flannery' poemed
a mimic of Afaa Weaver's "The Appaloosa"
in our safe home poetry class.

I think about this other time
at Starbucks,

when the wife of a colleague
leaned between
'Flannery' & me—

said, *Aren't you Jennifer?*
She came between me &
my notes, actually. The interview was over.

⋆

I don't tell
'Flannery' any of this. I stop her story—decide,

Next time,
let's talk in my car—

okay.

Why Aren't We Listening?
Amna Abdullatif

MEERA WAS A 14-year-old Indian girl in my class. She wore her long wavy dark hair pinned up from the sides to the back of her head with the length of it flowing down against her shoulders. She was quiet, with a shy smile, and would often sit on her own during breaks at school. The girls in the class would talk about her being 'odd', but no one ever said why they labelled her so.

We didn't have any classes together, and we weren't even really what I'd classify as friends—we rarely spoke. I knew she wasn't doing well in her classes; she was constantly being asked to register for additional sessions with teachers. Evidently the extra help wasn't really working because she didn't seem to progress with her studies.

I kept to a small group of close friends during high school, and I thrived in my classes. English was my subject of choice; I wasn't a genius by any means, but I could explain what needed to be done on assignments. I helped out most of my friends with their work, and they actually improved. Much to my amazement and theirs, some even did better than me! So, when Meera approached me to help her, I couldn't say no. I hadn't seen her ask anything of anyone before.

We sat together over a few lunch times, going over her work, and she was able to pick up the work relatively quickly. She would say thank you so many times that it grew tiring to respond with 'you're welcome' or 'no worries'. I think that maybe no one had ever helped her before without the expectation of something in return.

One day, as we sat over lunch to see what help she needed with homework, it was clear she was distracted and obvious to me that something wasn't quite right. There was something different in her eyes, in her inability to look at me. Her smile, which was often unshaken, was gone. I didn't understand it then, but it's clear to me now that the look in her eyes was fear.

Meera told me she had been sexually abused by her father for as far back as her memories could take her. Her eyes were firmly placed on the ground as she spoke. She skimmed over her own experience as if what she had endured was irrelevant or perhaps too painful to detail. The reason she was telling me was a call for help on behalf of others—her father had started to sexually abuse her 5-year-old twin sisters too.

I reassured her as best as I could, comforting her, listening intently, not making any judgments. I didn't want her to feel that what she was sharing with me was her fault or that telling me was a bad idea. But I had no idea if how I was supporting her was adequate for the horrifying reality of her experience. I didn't know what else to do. I felt that I needed to protect her in some way, but how could I? I was a 14-year-old myself.

I had high hopes for how our systems would support Meera. In my family there was a trust in the systems around us, I believed in our social and child protection services and our schools—I believed whole-heartedly that she would be listened to and protected by the adults whose job it was to keep her safe. That's the reassurance I got from my parents when I told them what Meera had said to me, and I wanted it to be true.

It was a Friday, and I knew I had to tell someone who could do something to help her. After school, I went to speak to the head teacher and to my amazement she didn't seem surprised. In fact, Meera's family had been of interest to social services for a number of years.

My head began to spin with so many questions.

If they knew, then why was Meera still living with him? And why were her sisters still there too? How could they not help her?

I couldn't understand how it was possible that these services, meant to protect children like her and her sisters, had done nothing.

I had to sit by the head teacher's office and write down the details of what Meera had shared with me. After completing that task, I was thanked for reporting it and told I could go home. I was never informed of what might happen or of what did happen.

That weekend was possibly the longest weekend of my life. It passed so slowly as I worried about what might happen to her and whether I did the right thing. On Monday morning, I was eager to see her. I wanted to make sure she was okay and that something had been done to take her and her sisters away from their father.

But she looked worse.

Defeated.

Sad.

She refused to speak to me.

Perhaps I was wrong to trust adults in power?

I believed that it was enough for Meera to share what was happening to her and for it to be taken seriously. That Meera would be taken out of the abusive home in which she lived; that the people who were meant to help would help; that she would be listened to, believed, and protected; that the man who was abusing her and her sisters would be punished. But instead, nothing changed for Meera in the two years of high school that followed, and I have no idea what happened to her after we finished high school.

Perhaps this is what still haunts me today—not knowing what happened to her after high school, and the powerlessness of being a young teenage girl trying to help but feeling like I failed.

What she shared with me changed my life and ignited a rage inside of me about how much silence surrounds abuse against children in their own homes.

Meera wasn't a special case or a rarity. In that same class, Sarah was self-harming and everyone knew about it. Unlike Meera, Sarah came across as confident. She was loud and chatty and would speak to everyone.

Like Meera, Sarah had been sexually abused by her stepfather throughout her childhood, and her coping mechanism was to self-harm. Her arms were covered in scars, and she would eloquently talk about what it felt like, to feel that pain, and know it was hers to control.

She was always absent and skipping school, often just to smoke and hang out with her friends in the woods in the back of the school. When I wanted to get out of geography classes, she was the one I'd 'bunk off' with to chat.

It wasn't surprising that she was really falling behind schoolwork—she made no effort throughout much of the time I knew her. But when we neared our final exams for high school, something changed and suddenly she was beginning to take school seriously, choosing to revise with us instead of meeting up with the older guys she knew. But as we got to the exam dates, the pressure from these men who she had started to ignore had become too much. In the end, they were offering to pay her money to come and have sex with them, and she chose that over doing her exams.

Again, even though Sarah openly talked about some of what was going on in her life, there didn't seem to be anyone helping her out of the situation she was in. No one was paying attention to her or how her vulnerability was being exploited by older men.

Knowing Meera and Sarah made me question the systems we have in place to keep children safe—the very same systems that have long been fought for and continue to be fought for to hold sexual predators and abusers to account for their crimes.

Why aren't we listening to what children are telling us?

Why are children still disempowered and broken by the systems there to protect them?

Over and over again, abusers are getting away with crimes. Those crimes stay with survivors for the rest of their lives, with little to no support to overcome those experiences.

Now as an adult, I understand that we are the ones who want to silence children for the experiences and abuse they endure. Even when they are sharing their pain with us, we don't seem to be able to hear it fully and enter into a conversation with them.

Survivors are punished for the crimes of others as the people they tell get uncomfortable listening to their experiences. We can't seem to deal with the details of their experiences. The complexity of the issues and the depth of the pains are too difficult for many of us to comprehend.

We don't want to hear that 90 percent of sexually-abused children are abused by someone they know because that makes it so much harder to fix with the systems we have. For many, like Meera and Sarah, it happens in their own homes by their own family members or other adults they are close to.

The survivors who speak out, who break that silence, who share their story, are too often seen as fragile in the eyes of those who know the scars they have to carry. We tip-toe around them, uncertain of how to respond. We fail to see the courage and strength of their survival and coping. In our blindness, we risk defining them by what they have experienced. Despite our best of intentions, this is our impact.

It is no wonder that one in three children remain silent, telling no one about the abuse.

But we can change this statistic.

Many of us have come across girls like Meera and Sarah, who sought us out to ease their pain by sharing their stories. I want us to be proud of the role we played as listeners, regardless of how small it seemed or how powerless we felt. It is a privileged position to be someone that others trust and know they can rely on for support.

While it can feel like we can't make a difference if not able to take away the pain or change the circumstances of someone's life, we were chosen as *confidantes* for a reason. They were able to see our empathy, kindness, and warmth. Our ability to listen and hear them is a comfort to the pain. They will always remember that, and remember us.

Meera and Sarah displayed a courage that I hope many of us learn from.

They are survivors.

They broke the silence around the abuse they carried all through their childhood. Even though I felt then, and still feel now, that I let them down in not being able to fix their situations, I know that it was an important step for them to trust someone to be able to let go of that silence that surrounded them and surrounds so many children who have experienced sexual abuse.

Meera and Sarah trusted me with their stories, and their stories changed me. I hope on some level that sharing with me created a space for them to build up their resilience and healing. And I know, for me, knowing their stories made me a better listener, advocate, and ally. We all have the power to do that within our peer groups, regardless of our age.

Let us honour the stories that are shared with us in order to create the necessary change we need to break the silences around us.

Unintended Consequences
Lauren Spahn

I SIT. FOR SIX-HOUR BLOCKS, three times a week. And I wait.

I wait for the phone to ring.

Sometimes nobody calls. Sometimes, it seems like there's not a moment to catch my breath in between the end of one call and the ring of another. Sometimes my heart is left heavy. Sometimes I'm filled with anger. Sometimes I'm profoundly confused. Always, I'm inspired. Inspired by the power of the voices I hear and the courage of those who are speaking.

As a volunteer on the county's only sexual assault crisis line, I never know what is going to be on the other end of a call. Domestic violence. Homelessness. Incest. Addiction. Tears. Sometimes even silence.

Do I feel equipped to handle all of it? Absolutely not. But I'm continually reaffirmed, with each call, that the simple act of listening on the other end of the line makes a difference. Listening is how a voice is heard, held, and honored. Listening can bring truth to life. Listening invites the possibility of healing. This potential for healing lies in the opportunity for the speaker to uncover their own inner strength and wisdom as they share their story.

Healing is a journey; a deeply personal yet profoundly collective process. And every caller is at a different place on their own, unique pathway to discovering wholeness and peace in the aftermath of trauma. My role, as I've come to understand it, is to meet each of them exactly where they are on that journey by listening.

But when it comes to a phone call with a stranger, listening deeply in this way can be a challenging task. There are minimal contextual clues. No eye contact. No body language. No facial expressions. No environmental factors. Zero visual indicators. Just a voice on the other end of the line. So, I simply give my full presence, attention, and awareness to the person on that other end of the phone. I suspend my own opinions and judgments and, in doing so, hope I give the callers permission to do the same with their own. I tap into that space within me that has felt hurt, neglected, empty, alone, ashamed, guilty, afraid, confused, victimized, manipulated, angry, numb, or whatever other emotion is being expressed by the caller. And in feeling that shared emotion, I am able to connect with compassion.

I have come to believe that this compassionate listening is an art. It strikes me that my relationship to the art of listening parallels that of writing. Common advice, if you're seeking to become a better writer, is to dedicate time to writing every day. Even if what comes out is a list or incoherent sentences, it is in our practice that we grow as writers. My practice of compassionate listening feels similar in many ways. So, while I've received various iterations of training in this art, the root of my confidence lies in my daily practice of the craft.

This is all to say that, when it comes to listening, I feel practiced and, therefore, equipped.

With one major exception: minors.

When it comes to minors, I feel overwhelmingly ill-equipped to offer the compassionate listening I know is truly needed. Why? The answer, as I see it, is both vastly complex and utterly simple: mandated reporting.

As a California-stated certified crisis counselor, I am mandated to report any incidence of sexual allegations in which any party is under 18 years of age. And I am not alone in this mandate. All doctors, therapists, nurses, and teachers are also mandated reporters. Essentially, the majority of adults who classically interact with children and teens within our public and private institutions are required by law to report all the information disclosed to them about sexual assault involving minors.

On the most basic and straightforward level, this mandate makes perfect sense. It was designed and implemented with the intent to protect children – as individuals who are dependent upon adults for survival – from sexual abuse, misconduct, and manipulation. The beauty of this intention is that it acknowledges the dynamics of power that exist between adults and children and, from that place, aims to establish a system that will hold that power in check and offer justice to those who suffer at the hand of that power. So, when I get called to offer support to a family as their 8-year-old daughter is interviewed by law enforcement about her recent disclosure to a teacher that her grandfather fondled her genitals two nights prior, I feel immensely grateful for the mandate.

The more complicated shadow, however, shows up when a young woman calls the line seeking to better understand her options and process her experience of trauma. Like many callers, she hesitates, wondering aloud where she should begin. But when she says, "I was at the varsity basketball game on Friday night..." I take pause. Through the emerging pangs of guilt and obligation, I muster the voice to interject: "I'm sorry to interrupt, but I want to let you know that if you're under 18 years old, I am obligated by law to report any information you share with me and I want you to have

the choice to continue or not knowing that information..."
As silence fills the line, my heart sinks. Her inner conflict is
palpable in lack of voice, only breath; then I hear the click.
My inner conflict seems to pick up from where hers dropped
off, as I follow protocol and report the very little information
disclosed to me. It is in situations like this that mandated reporting can beget silence. For this young woman, and many
others, my mandate to report serves as a barrier to engaging
in a foundational foothold of the healing process: a safe and
confidential space to share their experience of trauma with
someone whose primary interest is to listen with compassion
and bear witness to their suffering.

While guilt certainly shows up for me in these moments,
I remind myself that the silencing of minors that mandated
reporting cultivates is simply an ingrained systemic barrier
and not a reflection of me nor any other individual within
the system. Quite the contrary, actually. I am continually
inspired by most of those with whom I've interfaced in this
work. Many law enforcement divisions have a remarkable
team dedicated to sexual assault and domestic violence. In
fact, most divisions employ advocates whose primary role
is to offer support to survivors as they navigate the criminal justice system. All medical rape kits administered in
the state of California are budgeted and paid for by local
police departments and, in those circumstances, the nurse
examiner (who is forensically trained), an advocate (which
all survivors have a right to), and law enforcement personnel
(officers and detectives) work together as a Sexual Assault
Response Team (SART). In my experience, most of these
team members orient to this work as being of service to the
community and see their role as upholding justice on behalf
of the survivor.

The barrier, as I see it, is grounded in the framework
of our criminal justice system: that one is innocent until
proven guilty. Justice, in this context, is rooted entirely in

the punishment or retribution of the perpetrator. And while we certainly don't want innocent people being put in jail based on accusations alone, a system designed in this way drastically fails to honor the experience of trauma and the need for healing. Not only is space not held for the personal reconciliation and healing of the survivor, but the tunnel vision created by the legal proceedings often disregards the healing process entirely for all parties involved.

This rigid structure within the criminal justice system, in turn, demands that individuals within the system (such as law enforcement officers or nurse examiners) follow strict protocols and questioning that prevent them from being able to meet the survivor where they are in their own healing. Their role is primarily to determine whether or not they can collect enough information to craft a viable case against the perpetrator (all sexual assault cases go to court as the state versus the perpetrator, as opposed to the survivor versus the perpetrator) and, secondarily, to collect enough overall data to be able to identify repeat offenders in the community. While this macro-level framework plays a valuable role in the safety of our communities, more often than not, it fails to align with the natural order of healing.

For those of us who are adults, these systemic dynamics do not have to dictate our course of action. For some of us, seeking justice through the criminal justice system will play a vital role in our healing journey, even if that process is slow moving. But for many, the pursuit of legal proceedings remains out of our control, requiring us to make peace and discover justice in other ways. But in either case, we can choose to seek counseling or pursue our own personal pathways for healing at our own pace. The reality is that for each of us as adults, when, where, and how we engage in that system will vary dramatically. Whereas, for those who are under 18 years old, this choice is pigeon-holed.

So, when I get a phone call one day from a mother whose 16-year-old daughter's best friend disclosed to them both that she was raped by a guy in their class the previous weekend, and she wants to know where the survivor can go to receive counseling, I feel stuck. My first instinct is always the same: to ensure that the survivor is presently safe. But once I confirm that information, I feel obliged to share with the concerned mother that I am required by law to report any information that she shares with me moving forward to Child Protective Services who, with enough information, will engage law enforcement in follow-up. The mother, naturally, is hesitant to strip the agency of this 16-year-old girl to make that decision on her own, as am I.

I proceed to share a handful of resources that the mother will be able to give to the survivor, including a support group and a clinic where she can get free testing for sexually transmitted infections without disclosing the incident, but I remind her that any counselor, nurse, or physician, like me, will be mandated to report. "So if she wants to get a pelvic exam, but isn't yet ready to engage law enforcement, she'll need to lie about what happened?" she asks me. "Yes," I reply, feeling like I'm yet another agent perpetuating this culture of silence.

I wrap up the conversation by reminding her that she is playing a huge role in the survivor's healing process by holding a safe space for her to share her experience. And in that role, she is poised to support the survivor in working through the fears that show up around engaging law enforcement. I try to instill in her the faith that working alongside law enforcement in this capacity has resurrected within me so that she may pass it forward to the survivor.

But in the end, I still feel ill-equipped. This is our reality. This scenario, and so many others, reflect the lived experiences of people who call the crisis line seeking to process, to navigate a complex system, and to be heard. It begs the questions: How can we orient our systems of justice towards healing and reconciliation? How do we honor the power of voice and bolster those who are discovering the courage to speak? What might the world look like then?

The Surprise That Surprises No One
Michelle Bowdler

TWENTY YEARS AFTER a violent home invasion so terrifying I could barely function, until I could again, the memories returned. Their reawakening stunned my nervous system, and I spent many a day feeling that there was still a knife at my throat. I got help and began to understand I was not alone. Unprocessed memories too overwhelming to feel at a moment of terror have to go somewhere. Think of them like a cancer that goes into remission—not ever truly disappearing but lying in wait, finding a way to pop up at the most inopportune time.

The Boston Sexual Assault Unit was formed in July 1984, a week after my attack, the last of a series that summer. The unit was formed so that police departments in neighboring jurisdictions could coordinate efforts in identifying if there was a pattern to the multiple break-ins and rapes terrorizing women across the city.

Decades later, I learned my case was never investigated.

And it was never solved.

After more than half of my life spent working to help women find justice for their rapes and sexual assaults, I yet again shout to the world #MeToo and look this time for change. What will happen this time? Will we be seen? Will we be heard? Will these crimes be taken seriously? Will perpetrators be held to account and see even a modicum of consequence?

SOMEWHERE IN THE CITY of Detroit sat an abandoned warehouse. Birds flew in and out of open windows, the floor littered with stray feathers and rat droppings. Long ago, its thermostat broke and what lay stored inside became subject to temperatures that sweltered past 100 degrees in summer, and dropped below freezing in the cold Michigan winter. Inside the building sat boxes stacked from floor to ceiling, filled with forensic evidence. Over 11,000 untested rape kits were discovered there a few years back, each representing a person who, on one of the worst days of their lives, submitted to a multi-hour intrusive physical exam hoping it might help identify their rapist. For the 11,000 human beings that each of those uninvestigated cases represented, no call ever came. Worse still, when the city finally began to go through these old evidence kits, they found matches to serial rapes that would have been prevented had they tested them sooner.

What happened in Detroit was no anomaly; human rights groups identified cities that ignored rape evidence over *decades*—Dallas, Los Angeles, Cleveland, Memphis, Las Vegas, Houston, Milwaukee, New York City, and dozens more. Estimates of close to half a million evidence kits that held DNA of violent criminals simply had never been tested. They were disregarded, shelved, and left behind.

Those kits were gathered from the private folds and spaces of women whose bodies themselves had been transformed into crime scenes. I remember all too well my own visit to a Boston emergency room in the mid-1980s—overwhelmed during the hours of questions and physical intrusion. Rape victims in cities around the country went through this procedure, many of us still in a state of shock, most likely expecting that the evidence collected be used in the service of identifying and convicting the perpetrator – or in my case, perpetrators – who committed unimaginable violence against us. The hundreds of thousands of untested rape kits exist because hundreds of thousands of us agreed to submit to a procedure consisting of head and pubic hair combing; vaginal, anal, and oral swabbing and retrieval of saliva, blood samples, and fingernail clippings, taken carefully under a bright light of an emergency room by strangers, following a violation that defines vulnerability. We had an internal exam performed. We may have had blood drawn and been given medicines to prevent sexually transmitted infections and had pictures taken to document bruising. We could have stayed home, choosing instead to be comforted by someone we felt safe with. But we did not. We went to the hospital and had this procedure done for a reason. Try to imagine learning that absolutely nothing had been done with your rape kit except to treat it like useless trash. Some cities stored them untouched for years, some decades. Others held onto them for a while, and then threw them away as unsolvable cold cases, as if the aging evidence became useless all on its own. My kit, in Boston, got thrown away.

As each of the hundreds of thousands of us, rape survivors, tried to rebuild our lives with no news, the question of whether we would ever receive justice for the crimes that had ravaged our bodies and souls went unanswered. When cities began attending to their untested kits, rapists were identified, but often the statute of limitations had passed; prosecution was no longer possible.

The most recent wave of news about sexual assault, harassment, and abuse of power along with the perpetrators' weak apologies and promises to get help is, simply put, more of the same. The list of famous – and ordinary – men who experience no consequences for their crimes is beyond commonplace. It is the rule rather than the exception. They almost always walk away from the accusations with far fewer scars to life and liberty than those they hurt. Just look at the current occupant of the White House.

In the United States, rape is the most under-reported felony and the least-successfully prosecuted. Victims are routinely disbelieved and our pleas – first for the rapist to stop and then for law enforcement to seek justice – are ignored. So, how do we survive in this environment when we perceive a clear message all around us that what we went through does not matter?

Rape, in this country, is not treated as a crime of brutal violence but rather as a parlor game: his word against hers, regret sex, revenge against a scorned lover. It's a game of denial and blame, of 'it didn't happen'; 'she's unstable and everyone knows it'; 'she just wants attention or maybe money'; 'she wants to destroy his life'; 'she is part of a well-crafted political conspiracy to discredit'. These tactics might be laughable if they didn't work in silencing us so much of the time.

Given all this, it seems fair to ask whether rape is actually a crime.

The fact that we even have the phrase in our vernacular *he said/she said* – as if it's as likely as not that a woman would lie about sexual violation – is itself telling about where this crime lives in our culture. If you have ever had a rape kit done or tried to report a rape to the police, you understand it is no one's idea of a good time.

Describing in detail sexual humiliation and violence is not something a human being would choose to do if they had any other option. If asked, what would public safety officials say about why so many crimes of rape were not investigated? How would they explain the wholesale abandonment of DNA evidence that could solve these violent felonies? What words of repair could they offer to the hundreds of thousands of women who sit silently in shame and despair, wondering if anything will ever change?

As my wife once said to me on a day my own intractable memories grabbed me hard, "You aren't crazy; what happened to you is crazy." On days when it seems we still have so much work to do, I try to believe that our efforts to speak truth to power do and will continue to matter. I still have to believe change is possible. I have to believe that this time, with the resurgence of women's voices demanding change, a reckoning toward justice will occur. Otherwise, it is simply too crushing.

This is why I will tell the story of the Detroit warehouse and the hundreds of thousands of untested rape kits nationally and my own story long after when it seems the tipping point must surely have been reached. We must try to help nudge the needle toward justice for rape survivors, beginning with demanding that victims are believed, rape is investigated, and perpetrators held accountable. Our flawed world has not yet made any of this easy for us, but we must continue to try. Every voice that refuses to be silent – whether it's a day, a month, or over thirty years after the moment they were victimized – tells us so much more than the violence done to them. It tells us about the world we live in, where freedom is a concept given only to a select few, and the right to sovereignty over our own bodies is not yet secured.

Community Of Silence
Ashley Easter

IT WAS A WARM DAY when I sat on the picnic bench outside of the church. The pastor had agreed to meet with me to hear about my upcoming event to support sexual abuse survivors and educate church leaders on preventing and responding to sexual abuse. I was nervous. I had several dismissive and painful experiences with pastors in the past relating to my own abuse story and my efforts to address sexual abuse in faith communities.

I introduced myself and thanked the pastor for taking the time to meet with me. I showed him a promotional video and an event flier. And just as I began to launch into my pitch about the tragedy of abuse in the church, he abruptly stopped me.

"You don't have to convince me," he smiled. "I already know this is a big problem in the church, and I support you and your work 100 percent. What can I do to help?"

I was honestly taken aback. In my experience, most pastors do not want to touch the abuse issue with a ten-foot pole, but this pastor seemed different. For the next hour we had a wonderful conversation. We talked about the pain of pastors protecting abusers, the way gender equality is important to ending sexual abuse, and the importance of pastors connecting survivors with professional resources like therapists and law enforcement if they would like to seek legal justice.

The pastor enthusiastically invited me to promote the abuse awareness conference, helped me make connections with survivors, and invited me to a special pastors-only prayer meeting to speak with local clergy about my event. This invitation seemed like an answer to my own prayers, as pastors were the exact group of leaders I wanted to meet with to share about the conference. He told me that he would strongly encourage the pastors to attend my event and that he believed a large number of them would attend.

Throughout the conversation I felt safe enough to let my guard down and trust again. "I finally found a pastor who gets it!" I told my husband when I got home. And truly, I believed I had found a safe person, a new tribe of faith leaders after so much pain from previous pastors.

For several weeks, my new pastor friend promoted me and the conference to his friends, colleagues, church members, and at religious gatherings. He rallied around me and shared disdain for abuse and support of my efforts to stop it.

But, in a moment, everything changed.

Just days before I was scheduled to speak at the pastors prayer meeting, I got a call from my pastor friend who had invited me. He told me he was revoking his invitation.

He told me that the other pastors had gotten wind that I believed in equality for women and promoted this as part of the solution for ending sexual abuse. The other pastors did not believe in equality for women and did not teach this to their congregations. They were angry that I would suggest equality as a solution to abuse. My pastor friend told me he could not allow me to speak to the other pastors because they would become 'hostile' towards me if I attended the prayer meeting. But what was even more devastating was that he immediately started backtracking on some his own former support of equality for women.

I could feel the energy between us changing as he spoke. It was like receiving a punch to the gut.

He went from fully supporting me and the conference to holding me at a distance while bending to the opinion of a pastor group he described as 'hostile' towards me.

What was happening? How could everything have changed so quickly? I thought I had found my people. I thought I had found my tribe. How did I so quickly become the enemy?

HUMANS ARE HARDWIRED for connection, community, and belonging.

Researchers John T. Cacioppo, Brené Brown, John Bowlby, and others have observed that being a part of a community has been key to the survival of our species for thousands of years. For our ancestors living in uncharted land or in volatile times, to be separated from the protective collective of a tribe often meant certain death.

As a means of survival, human beings developed the practice of living in like-minded and like-visioned groups. Strength in numbers protected clan members from other groups who might have desires for the same (limited) resources. In addition to physical and provisional protection, human beings found emotional security in the shared vision of the group. Anyone who dared to harm a fellow member of the clan, threaten the methodology of the group, or risk the resource supply would have the whole of the community to reckon with.

While we do not have all of the same concerns as our ancestors did, we are still designed for connection and tend to gravitate towards insular communities. It is easier, and often feels safer, to remain in groups with people who act and believe just like us. Tribes, clans, and/or groups define belonging: who is in and who is out, who is safe and who is a danger to the community.

We see this polarization within the political realm. A political party leader may commit a grave mistake, but their party will still back them. On the other hand, if the opposing party leader commits the same mistake, the incident is weaponized against them. Nuance and conversation go out the window. Valid points of criticism are discounted and quickly shut down. All efforts are made to protect the integrity of the group.

The church is another place we often see insular clans with a distinct 'us against them' mentality. Whether between churches and the secular world, churches and other religions, between denominations within Christianity, this tribal mentality goes back for centuries and horrific events – from the Inquisition to the Crusades – document its impact.

Some churches are stuck in the mentality that only they and their associates know and represent the truth. Any differing beliefs or criticisms of their community are seen as a direct attack and a danger to the safety and existence of their particular beliefs.

LOOKING BACK NOW, I think an unhealthy tribal mentality caused my pastor friend, and the community he was bringing me into, to back away from me.

When these pastors realized I believed in equality for women – a belief that went against their interpretation of the Bible – they saw my efforts as an attack against their church's reputation rather than as a critique for the safety of their female congregants. They saw me as a danger to the existence of the group as a whole, and this is what caused them to be 'hostile' toward me. If I pointed out a flaw in their ranks, it could give 'fuel' to opposing groups and could even cause a reduction in their own members. So, I was made out to be the enemy—an unchristian, unsubmissive, rebellious outsider.

Sadly, this was not the first or last time I would experience shunning by a community like this. Not only have I experienced this type of pain when working to support survivors within their church communities, but I have also experienced it in relation to my own story.

Recently, I listened to the brave abuse survivor, Rachael Denhollander, as she spoke up about the abuse she and hundreds of other women in the gymnastics community experienced from physician Larry Nassar. In that very public trial, the judge allowed Denhollander to give a speech at the sentencing hearing for Nassar (who will be spending the rest of his life in jail). She spoke out strongly against him, and she brought elements of her Christian faith into the conversation as she spoke of God's justice and desire for accountability for abusers along with her choice to extend personal forgiveness to Nassar.

After the trial and sentencing, the Christian world went wild—openly celebrating Denhollander's bravery and condemning Nassar's abusive behavior. Articles were written and statements were made supporting Denhollander's courage to speak up about the abuse. But then, Denhollander made a prediction. She predicted that the church's response would be quite different if she were to speak the same way about famous pastors who have been credibly accused of abuse by multiple victims or if she were to speak out against the churches who participated in covering-up the pastors' actions.

Sure enough, she was right. Given a national platform, Denhollander decided to use her fame to draw attention to an abuse scandal that had not been properly addressed within her conservative Christian community. She asked for accountability and an independent investigation of the ministry in question.

Immediately, the same Christian leaders who had been supporting her just days before turned and tried their best to discredit her publicly. They only wanted a vocal hero if that person was speaking out against those they did not have any relational ties too. Her criticism of the poorly addressed abuse in the church seemed to be taken as an attack.

This experience led Denhollander to say, "It is with deep regret that I say the church is one of the worst places to go for help. That's a hard thing to say, because I am a very conservative evangelical, but that is the truth. There are very, very few who have ever found true help in the church."

For me, Denhollander's words ring sad but true. From my own experience as a survivor and a sexual abuse victim advocate, I know that churches often side with protecting abusers or respond by wielding dangerous oppressive doctrines over victims. In in the aftermath of one of my own experiences, I was told by a pastor that speaking up would be putting a blot on the name of Christ. Somehow I knew – in that moment and now – that this doctrine really only meant the church leader was afraid for the reputation of his church community.

Brené Brown, says it well in her book, *Braving the Wilderness: The Quest for True Belonging and the Courage to Stand Alone:* "When the culture of any organization mandates that it is more important to protect the reputation of a system and those in power than it is to protect the basic human dignity of the individuals who serve that system or who are served by that system, you can be certain that the shame is systemic, the money is driving ethics, and the accountability is all but dead."

The Amish call it 'shunning'. Scientology calls it 'disconnection'. Other traditions call it 'church discipline' or 'excommunication'. No matter the word being used, it is extremely painful to be cut off or rejected by your community. And this is exactly what happened to me and so many of my survivor friends in churches that put the mission of church before the wellbeing of the people the institution claims to serve.

I have been treated as a danger to my faith communities for speaking up to protect myself and others. In some instances, this shunning and the ensuing emotional pain reached a point where I knew I had to cut myself off entirely from a group for the sake of my own healing.

I have been painted as a troublemaker and someone who was out to harm my community. Confusingly at times, I was also 'love-bombed' as the group tried to lure me back into their control. People have told me they were praying for me, that they still loved me but that I needed to repent. They said that the door was always open if I decided to come back but that to come back I would need to listen as they told me how sinful I was for my methods of supporting survivors.

I saw through the deception. I knew even if I 'repented' for using my voice that things would never be as they were before. Love-bombing, even if accepted, comes at the expense of your voice and agency. Whether I was deemed a messenger of Satan or a mission field to be won, I became distinctly aware that I was no longer 'one of them' and that was overwhelmingly painful.

I have lost childhood friends, loved ones, and entire faith communities I had invested years of time and energy into. While I knew I was no longer welcomed within these communities, and even while I knew it was not good for me to maintain connections there, I still felt the pain of those losses.

In the darkness of this grief, I longed for community. I felt both loss and a sense of withdrawn protection. I learned that these types of feelings, though painful, are part of the normal grieving process. I had to learn that it is okay to admit such feelings of loss even when the person or community that is lost was abusive or unhealthy. And now I know that eventually the pain lessens, it gets better.

Tribes, clans, and groups are not all bad. In fact, paradoxically, I believe that healing only comes in the presence of community. Healing community must, however, be distinctly different from groups that are based on exclusivity and control. Safe community will be defined by the principles of love, acceptance, empathy for others' pain, and a willingness to learn from differing points of view. Just as importantly, healing communities will value the protection of the weak and wounded over the collective 'brand' of the group.

Writing and speaking on the topic of sexual abuse has opened up a whole new community for me. I have had the privilege of connecting with survivors from across the world, sharing similar stories of abuse and the church's unholy responses. We have bonded over our shared pain, our similar experiences, our journeys towards healing, and our passion for ending abuse.

While it was a community that harmed me, it has also been a community that has healed me.

As I continued to speak out about my abuse, other abuse survivors began reaching out to me with similar stories. It resonated with me—the isolation and loneliness they were feeling as they left the communities that would not support their healing or entertain safety precautions. In response, I founded The Courage Conference, a yearly event to empower survivors of abuse (both Christian and non-Christian) and to connect them to safe community and healing resources. From day one, the event has been a success. Hundreds of people, many of them survivors, have experienced the healing that comes with face-to-face community. Truly, I have never experienced anything like it. There is something special about being in a room full of other survivors that overwhelms you with a feeling of not being alone. This camaraderie gave us the boldness to talk amongst ourselves about our abuse and our struggles to heal. Some of us spoke about our abuse for the very first time and others who had long since been void of community found a safe, connective tribe.

We've seen this practice on a larger scale with the #MeToo and #ChurchToo movements. There is something about a protective collective of voices caring for one another, saying 'you are not alone', 'we believe you', and 'we've got your back' that begins to undo the damage created by abuse and shunning.

I have come to realize that it is through connection with people that we begin to heal, whether that means attending a large event like The Courage Conference, becoming involved in the #MeToo or #ChurchToo movement, telling a friend, or reaching out to a licensed counselor.

It is paramount that the people and community we reach out to are truly safe. I look for the danger signs of isolationism, silencing of vulnerable and hurting people, and grandiose leaders within power structures. I look for community where questions and truth telling are encouraged and where boundaries are respected. Communities are only truly safe when the safety of people is placed above the reputation of the group's leadership and image.

Speaking up about abuse and healthy solutions was a moral decision for me. I realize not every survivor is in a place where they are able to share their story or work in victim advocacy, but I knew that I was. I wanted to protect others, and I knew that staying silent would only fuel the darkness of abuse that envelops so many.

I never regretted my choice. I know, for me, it was the right thing to do.

For those of us who have experienced the pain of rejection from our communities when disclosing abuse or pressing for responsible change, let us remember: we are not alone. I've experienced it, and so have the hundreds of survivors I have spoken with. I've come to learn abuse is never the fault of the victim and neither is rejection by a community in the aftermath of abuse.

Men's Work
Frederick Marx

"The mature Masculine must be reclaimed by
the modern world. Its virtual absence from tech-
nologically advanced societies has resulted in
one of the more serious moral crises ever to face
Western civilization... In our world, genocide
is barely noticed. Rape is used as an instrument
of both pathological male self-expression and
ethnic war...Violence is becoming the preferred
solution to interpersonal disputes. In all this,
we see evidence that mature Masculinity, in
its fullness, has all but been forgotten, and that
'Boy Psychology' is prevalent."

–Robert Moore & Doug Gillette
(*King, Warrior, Magician, Lover*)

IN 2008, I WAS ASKED to give a presentation to about
a thousand US Army Non-Commissioned Officers in
Washington. They had flown in from around the world to
attend a weekend workshop on ending sexual harassment
and abuse. The Army's stated goal was to end it within ten
years. They failed. Miserably.

But I don't fault them for trying. I was scheduled as the first speaker. After all the welcoming speeches by officials and politicians, we were running a half hour late. By the time I came to the podium, I was told to reduce my presentation from 30 minutes to ten.

I wanted to show clips from my film – *Boys to Men?* – that clearly illustrate ways in which masculinity formation takes place in teen boys. I wanted to explore how those issues play out in adult men and can impact them in relation to sexual harassment and abuse.

I couldn't do any of that in ten minutes. Instead, I said I wanted to address the men in the room directly. (Though the conference organizers were women, the audience looked to me to be about 98 percent men.) I basically told them that until they could feel their own feelings the likelihood was extremely small that they'd ever relate to or understand the feelings of sex abuse victims. I walked off to a smattering of polite applause and was not invited back to a similar gathering the following year.

I might as well have told the men that until you live on Mars you'll never understand Earth. Suppression of feelings is one of the key lessons every soldier is taught in boot camp. During battle time deployment, it is certainly true that feeling feelings can get you killed. Circumstances of life and death demand that soldiers make the best, most rational decisions they can in the moment. Though intuition can be extremely valuable at those times, accompanying emotions of fear, anger, sadness, and shame can be life-threatening. Training takes over, and normal mental processes are overridden by programmed autonomic patterns. But what's an invaluable modus operandi in wartime can itself become a killer in peacetime.

The problem is that human emotions are not faucets that can be turned on and off at will. Once we're trained by our parents, schools, workplaces, or the military to hide, repress, and deny our emotions, they don't come back with ease and facility when we need them. With them off, we will remain unconscious of that which makes us most human. Which doesn't mean they no longer exist. They're just driven underground where the danger of the truths they represent can be repressed. Then, when feelings arise in others, just like in ourselves, we can insist they be choked down, often with insults and judgments: *Don't be a pussy. Suck it up. Stop acting like a baby. Be a man!*

The latter judgment points toward part of the military problem. Women aren't 'man enough' to suck it up when they come forward with their stories of sexual harassment and abuse. That's their 'problem'. If they were 'man enough', their pain would be treated like all pains in the military—something to be ignored and dealt with privately. The military is not institutionally or culturally equipped to deal with the pains that the victims of sex abuse and harassment experience. The documentary entitled *The Invisible War* makes this painfully clear.

Still, my presentation didn't fall entirely on deaf ears. Women responded. During the evening reception, one woman told me privately she'd been waiting her entire life to hear a man say what I said. Other women also came up and thanked me. I don't recall speaking to a single man.

My own journey on the path of the mature masculine began when I was nine. My father died suddenly of a heart attack—he was 41 years old. I was in shock. On our way to the funeral, my uncle put his hand on my bony shoulder and said, "Well, Freddy, you're the man of the house now."

Nowadays we might laugh at the inappropriateness of such statements. But his words didn't seem inappropriate to me. I wanted to be that man, to care for my mother, older sister, and younger brother. I wanted to live up to that responsibility. I thought my father's death and my uncle's recognition somehow combined to anoint me a man. It would be many years before I understood the childish conceit of that idea. I was no more a man than my sister or brother or mother. But that moment planted a seed in me, one that would continue germinating throughout my lifetime. How to become the man of integrity and honor I yearned to be? How to hold responsibility for the wellbeing of those I love? What, in fact, is it to become a man?

There followed many years in which my dad's name was never spoken in our house. I drove all my questions and fears inside and never once had a conversation with my siblings or mother about my dad. Silence became the norm. Though the term didn't exist for another 15 years, I essentially grew up with post-traumatic stress. With my peers, whenever they asked about him, I simply said he was dead. That ended the conversation.

Through my teen years, I drank, did drugs, and somehow managed not to kill myself or harm others. No men materialized to show me how to become that man I wanted to be. Coaches, neighbors, relatives, certainly not my uncle... no one offered me that much-needed mentorship. Though I had good friends and a supportive social circle, I felt alone, hermetically-sealed by the silence I couldn't articulate or name. It was only a matter of time before I acted out.

The one and only time I ever hit a woman was when I was 18. My girlfriend and I were in Jamaica. I was masking my fright at this strange, new world behind bravado. 'The Third World' we called it then—low-income people of color with ways foreign to me. I needed intimacy and wanted reassurance, but I wasn't conscious of it and didn't know how to ask for it. So when my girlfriend was her usual social self at a party one night, talking with numerous other men, my frustration and jealousy boiled over into rage, and I hit her on the shoulder. Once we got back to the States, we had the good sense to break up. The irony was we then only grew closer and became lifelong best friends.

I didn't know it at the time, but I was unconsciously drawn to the company of women and gay men. I felt my emotions were safe with them, and I could risk being vulnerable. I unconsciously steered away from strong Type A males. I projected all the worst aspects of my father onto them, thought them arrogant, full of themselves, self-appointed leaders seeking obeisance. This pattern emerged in my teens and continued through my 30s. Though therapy in my early 30s helped bring awareness to some primal wounds, it succeeded only in helping me feel safe to open my heart to my therapist. I had no facility or interest in opening my heart to the wider world, especially to men.

I was nearing 40 when I started 'men's work' and learned about emotional intelligence. I learned only then, as a heterosexual man, how to give and get love from other men. What led me there was purely intuitive. I sensed that I could benefit from being among the men. My brother had done the workshop and called me to recommend it. For the first time, I understood how even the toughest men are precious and tender if approached in the right way. I learned that being vulnerable not only proves you're courageous, it opens the door to others and makes deep relationship possible. I learned that my heart was my great gift to the world, not my intellect. I learned that my own silence was toxic and for my own survival and well-being I needed to articulate my feelings. My life was never the same.

Robert Bly, one of the godfathers of 'men's work', says American men are the walking wounded, unconsciously seeking their father's blessing. That was certainly true for much of my life. It was also a fair summation of most of the men I knew. The evidence of that wounding and of all that unconscious seeking is too great to recount here, though a great deal of my artistic life has been spent analyzing the issue. Suffice it to say that too many men are suspended adolescents, ruled by their fears and unconscious appetites, still trying to prove something to Daddy. Unfortunately – given the immeasurable extent of horrible consequences – those men largely run the world.

It's not a phenomenon limited to angry white male Trump supporters. At 17, by the time I entered college in 1973, I considered myself a feminist. I was raised by a feminist mother and, to a lesser degree of influence, a feminist older sister. Feminism, gender equality, and fairness all made implicit sense to me, along with all other forms of social justice—race, religion, sexuality, class. But even still, in lessons I learned during adolescence from my Mom, like "You need to learn how to be a good husband to your wife," there was always an implicit, if not overt, tone of shaming. "You need to measure up. You need to succeed where millions of other men have failed. Otherwise, you will not be good enough. You will be a failure."

My mother and sister never missed an opportunity to recount parts of the endless list of male crimes against women and girls, against humanity in general—the crimes of patriarchy. Were these statements accurate? Yes. Was it important for me to be aware of my male privilege? Yes. But was I somehow personally to blame for these earlier crimes? No. Was it my responsibility to carry shame on behalf of all men? No. Yet I was brought to feel it was my shame to carry by virtue of being born male. This instilled some resentment and fear in me around women. I didn't want to be shamed into being a better man. When they criticized my behavior, it just felt controlling. I didn't want to be controlled; I wanted to be inspired to be the best man I could be. I wanted to learn what is noble and good about being a man. That meant having mature masculinity modeled for me by emotionally open, psychically strong, virtuous men. Thanks again to 'men's work', this was something I finally experienced in my 40s.

But that was later. Back in my college days, I read Susan Brownmiller: "[Rape] is nothing more or less than a conscious process of intimidation by which all men keep all women in a state of fear." I also read numerous other feminists. Partly due to this education in feminism, partly due to the admonitions of my mother and sister, partly due to my natural shyness around attractive women, I never would engage in any behavior around women that might be construed as offensive:

- I would never say anything complimentary about a woman's appearance unless or until I got to know her very well—not clothes, not hair, not eyes, certainly not body shape, nothing.
- I would almost never touch a woman unless she touched me first or she explicitly invited me to.
- I would never open a door for a woman for fear of signaling some incapacity on her part. I would never offer to pay for something like a meal or a coffee for fear of reinforcing economic inequities or setting up unwelcome concerns about unspoken forms of repayment.
- Even when having sex with long-established lovers I would never assert strong 'top' behaviors unless I explicitly received encouragement or permission.

As I've seen times change over the years, and I've lessened my fear of causing offense and my willingness to carry shame, I have shifted some of these behaviors. I now view it as socially-acceptable to offer to pay for meals and movies, or to open doors. But I still default to steering clear of any topic in conversation, like compliments, that could be taken the wrong way. I used to think I was inept at flirting. Now I recognize that I simply refused to engage in it, occasionally because of intimidation, but mostly for fear of being offensive or considered harassing.

Long before I met my wife and fell in love, she sued the University of San Francisco for sexual harassment. She was harassed by her colleague in the English Department. I long marveled and applauded her for pursuing the lawsuit, given that she had only recently arrived on campus and was very much junior faculty. This was 1992. By suing, she effectively put her whole career on the line. Since she died in July 2016, I'm forced to speculate on how she might situate that action within our present historical moment of #MeToo and #TimesUp. What made her do it? What brought her out of silence into the open?

She had recently undergone a painful divorce from her first husband—a fine man, the father of her two daughters, but a man whose political and social views she could not reconcile with her own. Her teen daughters were coming of age and were less and less reliant on her care. In short, she was coming into her own as a woman and a professional, exploring emerging empowerment. But I suspect the lawsuit represented a major life shift for her because of an issue that went deeper. She was a victim of childhood sexual abuse from her father.

In 1992, when she filed the lawsuit, she might not have been even dimly aware of any connection between the two. But I see a connection and will venture to name it. She was speaking a resounding no—not only to the acts of harassment and abuse in themselves, but to social strictures that exile certain acts and speech to the realm of the unspeakable. She was liberating herself from a self-imposed culture of silence, a culture reinforced by her siblings and mother.

She never succeeded in getting her father to own up to his abuse, much less to make amends to her, and he was certainly never brought to justice. But by standing publicly at her university against any further form of sexual harassment, she was indirectly telling her father, and directly claiming for herself, a clear break with the past. *Never again.* Her life as a victim of sexual abuse was over. Though the lawsuit was a trial, anything but festive, undertaking it was her coming-out party. I'm sure her father got the message.

As individuals, we all need to reconcile our past with our present in our own ways and in our own time. But as members of institutions, whether the army or the university, we have a responsibility to, in a sense, protect spaces that promote emotional availability and encourage, rather than punish, vulnerability. Fortunately, life affords us endless opportunities to proclaim our truth and claim our wholeness even in the face of resistant and uncooperative institutions. When the dominant culture itself offers a window of opportunity like it has in this day, hopefully it will encourage that many more to seize the moment and say, "Now is that time. I'm ready to step out of the shadows of shame and self-recrimination and claim my autonomy, my wholeness, my agency." There are a lot of people open and receptive to that message right now. Who knows? Even the military might make room for it someday.

After The Freeze
Amy Elizabeth Paulson

I JUST WANTED TO FIT IN. To be liked. To excel at my job. I was an expert at pretending everything was okay. I was accomplished at numbing my pain. What I didn't know was how much these skills would be tested as a woman in corporate America.

He was a member of the Old Boys' Club (OBC). A former sailor in the Navy, David (not his real name) was tall, charismatic, and friendly—the kind of guy who always had a smile on his face and a twinkle of mischief in his eyes. Originally from New Orleans, he loved music and dancing. Company happy hours were just a dress rehearsal for a big night on the town.

It was my first real job working for one of the prominent 'Big 4' accounting firms. I had changed career paths from journalism to accounting, heeding my father's practical pleas: "Get a good, steady job so you always have something to fall back on."

I'd learned a little about women's issues in the workplace in undergrad. But wage gap statistics didn't paint a picture of how gender dynamics played out in real life. With all the naïve zeal and hubris of a 20-something fresh out of college, I figured I'd shatter the glass ceiling, rise to partner, start a foundation, make a difference for other women, and make my parents proud in the process. *Easy peasy.*

I hadn't even started my job yet when I realized that it might not be so easy. During my interview, the tax PIC (partner-in-charge) asked about our shared alma mater's football team prospects. "How do you think the team will do this year?" he asked. I was caught off guard. I'd rehearsed questions about my strengths and weaknesses and how I'd overcome challenges. But not about sports. I held my breath as beads of sweat formed on my upper lip. *Don't say something stupid.* "I think they'll do well if our star running back can stay healthy," I muttered, thankful in that moment for the hours I'd spent watching college football games, even if I didn't understand what was going on. He seemed satisfied.

Mental note: *learn more about sports.* I sighed, wondering for a brief second who I would need to become in order to make it in this firm—then quickly pushed the thought away. I wouldn't let this deter me. Several weeks later, armed with a handful of cheap suits and a brand new calculator, I arrived at the firm in early 2000, ready to take on corporate America.

David and I started our careers together as entry-level consultants, though he was much older than I, already married with two daughters. Occasionally, we'd walk to lunch in the warm, southern California sunshine, commiserating about how tough the hours were and how much it sucked to study for the CPA exam after pulling an all-nighter at work.

THE OFFICE POLITICS were tricky. At times, I felt like I was navigating an obstacle course while blindfolded.

At the top of the hierarchy was the OBC—my private nickname for the informal, cliquey group of men who ate lunch together, golfed together, talked sports together, and had each other's backs.

The leader of the OBC was our PIC—the same guy who'd asked me about football during my interview. During busy season, we worked mandatory Saturdays. "Be there at 8am sharp," I was warned by everyone in the office. "He gets there early. It's important to show your face." Beneath him were two other men in middle management—the kind of guys who, if you walked into their offices, would lean back in their chairs, hands clasped behind their heads, oozing confidence and ease. These three guys were conservative, white, and pillars in their church communities. They didn't drink, though got kicks out of hearing others' tales of drunken stupidity.

Below them were a handful of more junior guys whose careers were on the rise. They weren't ultra-conservative, and they certainly enjoyed drinks at happy hour. But something about them resonated with the top guys in the OBC. Apart from them, there were about twenty or so other consultants, ranging from senior leaders to newbies like me. It was clear: the rest of us weren't part of the OBC. David was.

He was a real 'guy's guy'. He was well-respected for his service to our country. He could shoot the breeze about all things sports. He was invited to golf with the guys. I was not. *Ironic,* I thought, *since I took golf in college, thinking that I'd need it for all those schmoozy business outings, yet not once did I ask myself whether I'd get invited to them in the first place.*

Out of a dozen or so partners in our office, only two were women. It wasn't a secret that they didn't have kids. Kids were why more women weren't partners—or so the rumor went. "You know Lisa (not her name) the senior manager who only works 80 percent?" one of my female colleagues whispered to me. "She's well-respected, has been here longer and brought in more clients than most others in the firm. But she'll never make partner. No one makes partner working part time."

Of the two female partners, one was never at the office—her name only uttered in reference to her coveted candy jar. The other was equally feared and disliked, known by a handful of unkind nicknames like 'Big Boobs', 'Duck Lips', and 'The Bitch'—referring to her affinity for plastic surgery and ripping new hires into shreds. I rarely had interaction with her apart from the odd disapproving look.

It was hard to hide my disappointment. I needed a mentor. Someone who would give me sage advice about how to navigate the stifling power dynamics of the OBC. Someone who, as a woman, would show me how to be myself, while reflecting back the strength and power that I couldn't see within me. I wanted to be assertive yet kind, respected yet approachable—while still being accepted by the OBC. Maybe this isn't possible.

My corporate zeal quickly wore off. I'd heard people talk about how I 'had promise' as a new hire, which made me content to continue playing the game. Underneath my bravado, I was desperate for approval. On the rare occasion that I found myself at lunch or waiting for the elevator with someone from the OBC, I'd make a sarcastic joke or reel off some sports trivia. After an uncomfortable silence, I'd clear my throat as crickets chirped in the background. I knew I was better off just being quiet.

ABOUT A YEAR into our new careers, we were at a company retreat. As a reward for surviving the harsh busy season, new hires in the region joined together for two days of camping and team-building. During the day, we'd kayak and mountain bike. In the evening, we'd drink beer and roast marshmallows.

It was late. Eyes half-closed and a sloppy grin on his face, he walked me back to the co-ed cabin we shared with several others who were already passed out, snoring in their bunk beds.

I heard him shuffling around in the pitch black as I dozed off in my bed. Suddenly, I jolted awake, startled by the feeling of someone behind me, his hands reaching around to the front of my waist, slipping underneath my sweatpants and into my underwear. He was in my bed. I wasn't sure how. The smell of his strong, spicy cologne identified him in the dark. The sour smell of his beer breath was hot on my neck. My stomach churned. Nauseated. Time stood still. Panic washed over me.

I froze.

Decades later, I would learn about the freeze response to trauma through my training as a trauma healing community educator. When fighting or fleeing aren't safe options, our bodies instinctively play dead. We don't get to choose. In a split second, the most primitive part of our brain chooses for us. Our cognitive brain shuts down, including the area responsible for speech, and we – quite literally – become silenced. Stress hormones numb our physical pain, protecting us from being overwhelmed by the present moment. This handy feature of our body's natural intelligence helps us cope in the face of trauma. Yet shame and guilt often follow.

Like many survivors of childhood sexual abuse, I discovered, freezing was automatic for me. I was only about 5 or 6 years old when I was repeatedly molested by a neighbor. Physically overpowered and unable to fight or run away, I'd freeze. Afterwards, I'd swear not to tell. Then, we'd pretend like it never happened. Until it did again. And again.

The cycle of freeze and shame became my go-to response in life. When feeling stressed or overwhelmed, I'd panic in silence, dissociate from the physical and emotional experience, and numb out with my agent of choice (food, drugs, and alcohol were favorites). Later, I'd feel terrible guilt. What I didn't know then was that each time I repeated that familiar cycle, I reinforced a neural pathway that made it harder to react any differently the next time. When digging a deep ditch, water has no choice but to flow down that path. My ditch led to freeze and shame.

Seconds passed slowly while I remained frozen in that cabin in the woods. Hearing the sound of others stirring in their bunk beds shook me out of my paralysis.

"Stop! Go back to your bed!" I hissed in a low voice, fearful of others waking up and jumping to conclusions if they saw him lying behind me, his hands in my underwear.

"Are you sure?"

"Yes!"

He jumped out and retreated into the darkness while I lay there scared, confused, and utterly disgusted. I slept little that night, obsessing over every interaction since we had first met: drinks at happy hours, tasteless jokes (his favorite was one about how a woman has legs so she won't leave a slimy snail's trail behind her), singing in the parking lot at the CPA exam. *How could this have happened? Was it my fault?*

Over the days and weeks ahead, I avoided him altogether. To my horror, he was still friendly, as if nothing had happened. *Did he even remember?* Every time I saw him walking near me, I'd pretend like I'd forgotten something at my desk and scurry away. His twinkling eyes and musky cologne made my skin crawl.

I knew what he did was wrong, far from consensual. Hell, I had even met his gorgeous wife and kids at the firm's annual family picnic. I'd thought he was a real friend. I'd confided in him about the ups and downs of moving to a new city without any friends, feeling like I wasn't playing the corporate game right. I felt betrayed.

But who would ever believe me? No one, I thought, least of all the OBC. It was a camping trip, after all. Everyone had been drinking that night. We didn't have sexual harassment training back then. What I knew I'd learned from the movies. It was only harassment, I thought, if someone much more senior threatened a woman with losing her job if she didn't sleep with him. This was not that. *Don't rock the boat. No one will understand. Just forget it. Be quiet, like a good girl.* So that's what I did.

I pushed the bad memories to the darkest corners of my mind and heart and poured my energy into work. Though I loathed being around him, I decided that being friendly was the best way forward, lest word start getting around that I wasn't a team player. Just like when I was a child, I pretended. I played nice. Years would pass before I'd recognize this pattern and have the courage to change it.

Then it happened again. This time to another woman.

A part of me wishes that I could tell the horrific story of what happened to her. Likely somehow it will validate my own experience. Or *his* shittiness. Because that's what survivors do. We shame ourselves into believing that we don't matter. That if it only happened to us, it doesn't matter because we don't matter. And then we silence ourselves. I did. For months. And then for years after that. Just like I did when I was a child.

But I can't tell her story because it's only hers to tell.

When I found out about it, I was in torment. *If I had reported what happened that night in the woods, would this have happened to her?*

The night it happened to her, he didn't go home, and he didn't show up to the office the next day. It had been a blow-out night of bar hopping, starting with a firm-sponsored happy hour, in the middle of our busiest season. His wife frantically called the firm to ask where he was. Someone remembered he'd gone to a hotel. When the office tried to reach him, a random woman answered the phone. He was warned: keep your personal matters away from the office.

It was all too much to process. I stewed in anger and guilt for days—until an unfamiliar feeling washed over me. For the first time since I was a 5-year-old child locked in the bedroom of my abuser's home, I felt strength. Or was it resolve?

I made the decision quickly, whispering the words out loud to a close friend before I could change my mind. Here was a small chance to take back the power that I had given away to others. Though I was scared, I feared more what would happen if I didn't say anything at all. I knew David would hurt another woman.

I sat on the phone, shaking in the little, private call room at the office, hoping to God that no one could hear me through the office walls as I reported everything to a kind, faceless woman from the HR hotline.

My biggest worry was backlash from coworkers. If they found out, especially if the OBC knew, I would be ostracized—branded as an overly-sensitive trouble-maker. These were the same guys who had made fun of me behind my back for wearing blue contact lenses. Asians don't have blue eyes, they scoffed (my Korean mother actually has beautiful, natural steel gray eyes). I imagined their harsh words of judgment in my head. This could be the ruin of my career—one that had only just begun. It was almost enough to keep me from reporting what happened.

"Don't worry," the woman on the phone assured me, "no one, apart from HR and the PIC, will know that you made this report."

Whew. The hard part is over.

Days later, I got a call from HR. David was given a warning. That was it. Not penalized or fired. Warned.

And just like that, everything went back to normal. For everyone else.

I changed departments and started commuting to Los Angeles, grateful that I would only have to see his creepy smile a few times a week. Later, I heard that the OBC invited him to teach a professional training, an unheard-of opportunity for anyone at the junior level. Tears of anger stung my eyes.

Feeling alone, I confided in a few trusted colleagues. "That sucks," they'd say sympathetically while giving me a 'don't expect me to treat him any differently' look. After all, this didn't happen to them. He was still a great consultant and friendly as ever. He was still invited to golf outings. Still Mr. Congeniality.

I was hardly Little Miss Proper—a fact that had played into my hesitation to make the HR report and that I fear led to the lack of indignation by my colleagues. I had hooked up with and dated a couple guys from work. Some colleagues still enjoyed teasing me for falling asleep on a luggage stand while waiting for the valet after a company event. I'd emailed the odd crass joke to a few colleagues. All of this weighed heavily on my conscience. I'd never heard terms like *non-consensual, victim-shaming, or minimizing.* Somehow, in my mind, I got what I deserved.

Finally, as if the universe were testing my rapidly-waning resolve, it happened yet again. One night after work, some colleagues and I headed to a nearby dance club. To my utter dismay, he joined our group. On the dance floor, I felt someone grab my waist from behind. I smelled that signature spicy cologne. My freeze response took over once again. As if in a trance, I swayed from side to side as my brain left my body.

He started grinding behind me, tightening his grip as his hands moved down to my hips. I felt something hard rubbing up and down against my butt and jumped around quick enough to catch a glimpse of his half-closed eyes and that sickening grin. "I have to go to the bathroom," I said as I rushed off towards the ladies' room then jetted out the back door. I caught a taxi and cried all the way home.

I WOULD EVENTUALLY LEAVE that firm and corporate America altogether. Nearly twenty years would pass before I experienced workplace harassment once again.

This time, it would take place in the social impact sector. Only he wasn't a colleague at my same level. He was a mentor. A Founder of a handful of well-respected, global social ventures. On paper, his track record told of a life dedicated to empowering women. In person, he was a confusing mix of misogynist comments and acts of kindness. Like David, he was charming, charismatic, and beloved by the community. He told perverted jokes with a wink and a smile. "Oh, that's just how he is," others would say.

Not surprisingly, he was staunchly opposed to the anti-harassment policies and education that I (and a fellow outraged colleague) had tried to implement at the professional networking conference he had founded. "These are isolated occurrences," he'd argue, referring to the handful of reported, and many more unreported, incidents of sexual harassment. "A policy won't change bad behavior."

For years, I brushed off his requests to drink wine together in front of the fireplace at his private apartment in the city. When he'd shower me with words of admiration or shyly ask if he could tell me he loved me, I'd look down and awkwardly thank him, feeding into it with a hug or a peck on the cheek. Red warning lights fired off in my gut, but my freeze response ignored them time and again.

A few times, I did speak up. Like after he confessed his jealousy of my husband. Each time he'd retort with a quick: "You know I'm just joking," then mumble something about his wife. Checking in with other women in the community, I wasn't alone. "Everyone knows that he loves being adored by younger women," they'd say. "That's why he always mentors them."

But, like the OBC at my old firm, he was untouchable. No one would dare call him out.

Then, I finally did. After seeing too many women suffer from harassment in the community, either directly by him or from the culture he normalized, I'd had enough.

I wish I could say that, decades after that incident in the woods, breaking the silence was easier. But, in truth, it wasn't. The stakes felt much higher: potential backlash from our shared network of social entrepreneurs whose communities around the world had benefited from his support, risk of personal and professional shaming, and possible loss of funding for my organization (whose very mission was to break cycles of trauma and abuse) which would ultimately mean a loss to the communities of survivors we served. Trying to add up all risks made me sick to my stomach.

And then I thought of all the women around the world, bravely sharing their #MeToo stories—from horrific tales of violence and abuse to nuanced narratives of gaslighting and power plays. I closed my eyes, took a deep breath, and drew strength from their courage.

With support from a witness on the phone, I confronted him. I laid out everything that was inappropriate, non-consensual, and just plain wrong. I made the distinction between his 'good' intentions to support women, and the painful impact of his words and behaviors. With calm assertiveness, I talked about the system of gender oppression, harassment, and harm that he, as a leader, had cultivated in our community, and the predators who took advantage of that under his watch. I admitted that I, too, was complicit in perpetuating that cycle by remaining silent. And, trying to hold the complicated duality of boundaries and compassion, I urged him to get counseling.

Then, I described what happened in the woods nearly twenty years before. This time, I said, I would speak out until someone put a stop to this.

Afterwards, a lifetime of tears spilled down my cheeks—not from anger or frustration but from a newfound sense of pride, relief, and hope. *This is what it feels like to stand in my power. This is what it feels like to be the woman that I had so desperately wanted as a mentor all those years ago.*

I heard a rumor that David was eventually fired from the firm after further incidents of harassment. I was both sickened and relieved. I wondered how many women he'd harmed over the years before the firm finally responded, and whether it was hard for those women to speak up too. I felt an instant bond with them.

The social impact leader resigned days after I confronted him. He made a public apology and reportedly started counseling. The organization he founded is working to implement stronger harassment-prevention measures.

Since then, I've opened up about my childhood sexual abuse. I've also spoken up to several men after witnessing them unintentionally perpetuate oppressive gender dynamics, whether against me or others, inviting a deeper conversation about the ways in which we all contribute to systemic inequity. And, even writing this piece has been a conscious action to step away from my old trauma response of freeze and shame and dig a new pathway towards grounded self-empowerment.

I know that my journey towards healing will never be easy. It's a daunting, often complex and painful road. But, it's also an inspiring and liberating one. And, after all these years, I'm now more hopeful than ever before.

Courage Calls To Courage
Emily Porth

I USED TO THINK there was a point in my life when I would be 'healed', when I had done so much work through talking about and processing my trauma that it would stop affecting my life. I would reach that point and never have to speak of my sexual assault again, having achieved the proverbial state where 'silence is golden' and my story would no longer trouble me or anyone else. And yet, every time I thought I was at the end of my healing journey and could not possibly have more work to do, or have more of my soul to bare, something happened to clearly indicate otherwise.

In April 2016, shortly after Brock Turner's legal case had been all over the media, I received an unexpected email from one of my first friends at university. Her message began:

> "I hope this note comes to you at the right time and place. It is certainly hard to write. I want to first of all say sorry to you for that awful Halloween when you were alone and raped. I was not well-equipped as a friend. I was not at the party but I was there when you got home and I have always wished I did more to support you. I remember feeling like what you were

> dealing with was bigger than us. Knowing what
> I know now I regret not talking about it more
> and I feel sick whenever similar stories are in the
> news. If I could go back in time I would not let
> you deal with it alone."

It is difficult to describe what it meant to read these words nearly 18 years after my sexual assault. I felt everything at once: relief, fear, validation, shame, love, gratitude.

In my friend breaking her silence about my experience, however, I also became acutely aware of the layer of silence that I had built in my present life around being assaulted. Fortunately, I was in the right time and place when I read her message and burst into tears, which gave me the opportunity to break my own silence. For the first time, I felt able to tell my husband that I was a survivor of sexual assault.

My story begins in September 1998, when I started my undergraduate degree. My mother had been the first person in my family to earn a university degree, and she did not begin her degree until I was eight years old. From an early age, I was acutely aware that universities were institutions of privilege and they were places that had not historically been accessible to my predecessors. In fact, I was so completely awed and intimidated by my professors when my classes began that I was too scared to speak with them and ask questions. I enjoyed my classes, though, and I was grateful to make friends quickly as a student living in residence. And then, late into my second month on campus, I was raped at a party.

I don't want to tell you about my assault. Despite no longer feeling like what happened was my fault, for me this story is still full of shame, despair, and rage. I've spent most of my adult life trying to forget what happened, even though, ironically, I don't remember most of the incident itself. There are several parallels between what the victim,

'Emily Doe', experienced in Brock Turner's case and what I went through during and after my own assault: I was also at a party, consumed a lot of alcohol, and passed out. In that state, when it was absolutely impossible for me to consent, a man raped me in front of his football teammates. The main difference between my situation and Doe's is that I knew my rapist, a man who I had gone out with a couple of times but never had sex with. What I do remember about that night is being inconsolable, being found by the friends who took me home, and knowing that 'something bad' had happened. My body knew and remembered, even though my mind did not. I was so desperate to deny and suppress what my body and instincts were telling me had happened that, to somehow normalise the situation, I went out with him again. He even teased me about still being a virgin, a topic that came up when we had first started seeing each other when I had been clear that I was not interested in having sex with someone with whom I was not in a committed relationship. No, it could not possibly be true. *Until it was.*

Several weeks afterwards, friends approached me with the details about what had happened. These details had come to light as the story trickled out, whispered in residence corridors by those who had witnessed my rape and by those who had seen me hysterical in the aftermath. These details, which had been blurry and disparate in the beginning, began to coalesce, and I realised I could no longer ignore the reality in which I found myself. Two friends came with me to his apartment on campus – I would not, and could not, have done that without them – and in my shaking, broken state, I confronted him. He admitted to us that he had raped me in front of his teammates without using a condom. And then my friends and I went to the police.

Encountering Emily Doe's story in the media leading up to my friend's email had been triggering, and reading Doe's victim impact statement was, in many ways, a pathway back into my own mind and heart around the time I was raped. Unlike Turner, my rapist was not ultimately charged with a crime, 'stripped of titles, degrees, enrolment', or compromised in his place as a university athlete. According to the police, this was due to the 'post-incident contact' I had with my rapist; I subsequently spent years feeling shameful about that contact until recently when I found out it is a common response amongst women who know their attacker within a social context.

After my rapist's confession I went to see a doctor on campus to get a pregnancy test and to be tested for sexually transmitted infections. The doctor was supportive and understanding, but when she offered to refer me to the counselling service on campus, I said no. After all, I didn't really remember the assault itself, and so my rational mind told me, "Of course you don't need counselling. There's nothing to heal from if you don't remember." But I didn't understand that my body still held the violence I had experienced; his confession had changed everything by forcing me to confront the reality that I had been raped. My experience with the police turned out to be a second assault. As Doe experienced, my rapist had taken away my worth, my energy, my safety, and my voice. The campus community and the police had taken away my privacy. After going to the police with me, my friends did not mention my assault again and, at that point in my life, neither did I. In reflecting back on this period and my silence, I wish I could slip back to early 1999 and have a solemn and heartfelt conversation with my younger self. Sitting down, taking her trembling hands in my own, I would tell her the infinite number of reasons why she needed to see a good counsellor immediately, rather than do what I actually did and wait nearly seven years.

You have no doubt heard other stories like mine, or perhaps even experienced something similar yourself. According to a 2015 report from the Canadian Federation of Students,

Emily Porth

"Many on campus sexual assaults occur during the first eight weeks of classes. More than 80 per cent of rapes that occur on college and university campuses are committed by someone known to the victim." The same report cited a 1992 survey in which a staggering 60 percent of the male college-aged students who participated in the study "indicated that they would commit sexual assault if they were certain that they would not get caught." It is also striking that violence against women in the context of men's sports is a subject of academic study. Given this context, it is worth asking what responsibility the university had in supporting me during this time. To my knowledge, most of the athletes from the football team were interviewed by the police. On that basis, I assume the university was aware of what had happened. However, I was never contacted by anyone from the university, and their silence is probably symptomatic of a wider issue: according to the same 2015 report from the Canadian Federation of Students, a full sixteen years after I was raped, only 9 of 78 Canadian universities had developed a policy on sexual assault. Everyone, from the university administration, to my peers in residence, to my friends, knew what had happened, but no one – aside from those two friends who came with me to report my rape – said anything. The silence itself was silencing. I spent five years on that campus consciously and subconsciously feeling anxious about unexpectedly running into my rapist, a fear that materialised more than once.

At the time, I don't think I found the university's silence to be surprising, and as I write this I wonder whether feeling daunted by the institution itself, right from the beginning, negated my expectation for any other outcome. Having been intimidated by my professors initially, after I was assaulted I had internalised too much shame and worthlessness to imagine creating any sort of protest as other survivors of assault on university campuses have done since. Emma Sulkowicz, for instance, used her senior thesis project in 2012 to make a bold political statement about the mishandling of her rape allegations by her university. Called "Mattress Performance (Carry That Weight)", Sulkowicz literally carried her dorm room mattress around campus with her for a year, including to her graduation ceremony. In reflection, though, I can see that I carried my own type of weight in the form of the pressure I put on myself to reach high academic achievement and in the way it affected every one of my intimate relationships moving forward. When one's formative experience of sex is so boundary-annihilating, the behaviours one regards as 'normal' in a relationship become blurry and treacherous. There were times in the following years when I put myself into risky situations that, in hindsight, were incredibly self-destructive and subsequently contributed to deepening my feelings of shame.

In the final year of my degree, I asked faculty members for letters of reference to support my applications to Master of Arts programmes. A senior male professor queried why my overall grade point average was low, relative to the high grades I had achieved in the last three years of my studies. Abashedly, I replied that I hadn't done very well in my first year, but I did not have the words to say any more than that.

During that final year, I took two courses in the Women's Studies Department. It was the first time I had really engaged with feminism, the deconstruction of gender norms, and had critically considered how women are represented in pop culture and the media. It was also the first time I had met other women who were willing to talk about the widespread sexual harassment and assault of women. I wish I had a journal from that time to help me reflect more specifically on what it meant to find a community of people who were willing to question all of these societal norms and advocate for gender equality, but I do remember that what I learned felt mind-blowing. In particular, I found it shocking to learn that so many other women had experienced sexual violence, and yet it helped to lessen the overwhelming burden of shame that I was still carrying.

As I pursued my Master's degree, overwhelmed by anxiety and insomnia, afraid I wasn't good enough to finish, I finally began to see a counsellor. For the first time, I felt like I had a voice and my story came tumbling out. This process left me absolutely shattered, and it was the beginning of a dark period of intense healing in my life. I was very fragile when I moved on to my PhD, and whilst still mired in a deep depression and coming to terms with my sexual assault, I became a volunteer in the women's centre at my new university. Watching my peers perform *The Vagina Monologues* for Valentine's Day was a turning point in my healing journey: witnessing women shamelessly embodying such powerful stories was utterly awe-inspiring, irreverent, and transformative. There had been a lot of jitters and excitement leading up to the performance, and I simply didn't understand why until I saw it. I remember my disbelief and joy that someone had not only written these stories, but that they were being performed all over the world. It remains the most stirring and impactful piece of theatre I have seen.

Around this time I met other women struggling through their advanced degrees. As we became friends and felt safe enough to become vulnerable with each other, it emerged that a startling number of us had experienced sexual trauma. Knowing these women, witnessing their courage to keep going, and being loved, trusted, and supported by them has immeasurably changed me. All of these encounters let me know I was not alone, and they lessened my shame and turned me into an advocate for women's equality and healthy sexuality. Neither myself, nor my friends, had the background, knowledge, or life experience to be this kind of advocate at the time when I was raped.

To receive an email from someone who had been a close friend during the period of my life when I was mired in pain and silence shortly after being raped, and to have her voice the same sadness and regret that I felt, made me feel like my healing journey had come full circle. The remainder of her email read:

> "If I could go back in time I would not let you deal with it alone. Which brings me to the letter from Joe Biden to the survivor of the Stanford college rape. He is right: this woman is going to change people's lives. I want you to know you are that person to me. The feelings of regret for not knowing to look out for each other and not knowing what to do afterward are my reminders to equip my son and daughter to know about rape, and to teach them how to be brave enough to not just intervene but to be in that awful shocking lonely space with a friend afterward. To offer solidarity and support. To understand that if someone assaults them it is not their fault. You are certainly not the only person I know to be assaulted but your choices to me have always been brave and smart. I just wish I said it at the time. Better late than never."

Although I had moved beyond blaming myself for my rape by the time my friend's email arrived, her perspective on what happened so many years ago helped to shift my thoughts and feelings in ways I had never before considered.

I had never thought of my choices as having been brave or smart.

I had never considered that the people who witnessed what happened to me and remained silent were still impacted by it, and that my rape influenced the choices they made for their own lives and families.

It helped me to understand that even if my friends and I had been silent about my assault for decades, we could still find our voices and share our stories, no matter what role we had taken in each other's narratives up to this point.

It made me realise that my story could still be powerful for others, even years after I had been sexually assaulted. That my story might be read by someone who had also been raped within a university community, and it might make a difference to them. That it might prompt someone to have an awkward, but crucial, conversation with their children about sex and consent. That it could give someone else the courage to email the friend who they knew had been raped years before and who they also weren't able to support at the time.

The title of this chapter is a reference to a quote by British suffragist Millicent Garrett Fawcett: "Courage calls to courage everywhere, and its voice cannot be denied." My friend's courageous choice to share the impact that my experience had on her and her life gave me the opportunity and courage to share my story with my husband. He read her email as I was crying, and then he held me. He didn't ask for any details, but he did say, "I hope that bastard got what he deserved!" His comment simultaneously made me laugh and cry. "Of course he didn't," I said through tears. But at that moment, the lack of justice was unimportant. It just felt good and healing to be known more deeply by someone I love.

I haven't really spoken further with either my friend or my husband about my assault since that time. But my husband knew I was writing this chapter, and he was there at the times when I walked away from the computer just needing a hug and a shoulder to cry on. In those moments, his unconditional support and reassurance required no words.

This new silence in my life is comfortable. Being silent does not mean being healed, but the silence itself is healing because it is wrought from vulnerability, rather than from shame. And, twenty years after being assaulted, it is better late than never.

Dissecting My Silence
Terrence 'Red' Crowley

"Lying is done with words, and also with silence."
—Adrienne Rich

SILENCE HAS A COMPLEX and paradoxical anatomy. In my own life, silence has been both an exquisite avenue of equanimity and peace of mind as well as a vicious guardian of my unearned privilege. In addition to its more ethereal qualities, silence has served to concretize my sense of entitlement as a man.

Enter Adrienne Rich and the fallout from the Montreal Massacre bringing an epiphany that forever changed me.

In the late '80s, a friend gave me a copy of Adrienne Rich's book, *On Lies, Secrets and Silence*—both a gift and a challenge. It certainly proved to be both. Although Rich speaks directly to women in her book, she is often talking about men and the requirement that women lie on our behalf. This mandate for distortion is to be carried out with words but often, and more insidiously, through silence. What I gleaned from her work is that silence, like all lies, creates faux relationships based on manipulation and characterized by control of others—the hallmark of male socialization.

Prior to discovering Rich, I had assumed in a rather unexamined way that my silence in the face of woman-hating behaviors served as a connection to men. Certainly it avoided conflict between us. After reading Rich's work, I was forced to come to grips with the fact that my conscious deception not only spawned power-over relationships with women, it also, quite unintentionally, impaired all my relationships with men to whom I was also lying. My silence connected me to male superiority and male privilege, not to other men.

While I grappled with the reality that my lying through silence was simply a vehicle for control of others, I simultaneously tried to hold in mind the long-reinforced male tenet that honesty and truth are the essence of manhood. I had assimilated dozens of variations on the supposed truism, 'A real man is only as good as his word'. What I was learning from Rich was that male honesty is a kind of empirical honesty: the Dow dropped 130 points today; the Broncos won 24-10. It is honesty about facts and figures, not feelings and affect. I was forced to acknowledge that we are baffled by even the prospect of relationships based on authentic affection. Instead, our honesty is confined to business, sports, and the degradation of women. Being aware of our emotional truth is not required of us. Quite the opposite, a stoic demeanor is the standard—my standard.

These were the ideas I was noodling around in my head in December 1989 when Marc Lépine entered an engineering classroom at the École Polytechnique in Montreal with a semi-automatic rifle and a hunting knife. He instructed the men to leave the room and then opened fire on the women, killing six, injuring three. He then moved through a corridor and into the cafeteria continuing his shooting spree. Before taking his own life, he killed another 8 women and seriously injured 10 others as well as 4 men. This event has come to be known as the Montreal Massacre. Lépine carried out the massacre because, in his words, women were taking jobs that rightfully belonged to men. He claimed that feminism equated to the ruination of the fabric of society and of his life, in particular. He had applied to the École Polytechnique in 1986, and again in 1989, but lacked several courses required for admission.

The country and the world were outraged by the murders. Several days later in an attempt to shake my sadness and rage, I attended a memorial service at the local Existentialist Church. The format was perfect. Incorporated into the service was the opportunity for everyone to express the depth of their feelings and take comfort in community. As I stood in the queue of 6 or 8 people waiting to speak of my anger and sorrow, the woman at the podium asked the rhetorical question: What would have happened if the men (some 50 of them) had refused to leave the room? When challenged by this question, I felt as if a sheet of ice water was thrown across my naked body. How cheap and hollow my horror and rage seemed in that moment. How often had I 'left the room' either literally or figuratively rather than stand shoulder-to-shoulder with women? Was my behavior substantively different from that of Marc Lépine or simply on a different part of the continuum of male controls over women? At that point, the podium was a platform for those who were truly willing to speak truth to power. I left the queue and slunk back to my seat where I pondered my many past silent transgressions for the remainder of the service.

I reflected on my silence as a young Army recruit in the midst of several dozen others, all of us bewildered by the new environment in which we found ourselves. There was a palpable awkwardness among us as we groped for ways to connect with each other in this strange, novel situation. In moments, we found our common bond: verbally dissecting women's bodies devoid of their personhood. While I congratulated myself on not joining in, I nonetheless opted for silence rather than confrontation for fear of being exiled from the inner circle of male entitlement.

I reflected on my tenure as a furniture maker, working under the tutelage of a German Master Craftsman whose bench was littered with photos of naked women in provocative poses. I said nothing for fear of jeopardizing a *primo* apprenticeship and a source of income.

I reflected on my silence at the health club when the guys joked of their desire to sexually assault one of the female instructors. To intervene would have cast me among those to be ridiculed. I was acutely aware of the inevitable alienation I would suffer and chose male camaraderie instead.

I reflected on my silence when my brother yelled, screamed, and cursed at his wife for not obeying his directives. She cowered and silently submitted, as did I, for fear of risking family ties and a connection to my brother's presumed wealth and power.

And on and on and on my silences go. My connection to male power and privilege, forged through my silences, consistently proved more compelling than the well-being of women. Taking the podium to speak of my own rage and sadness under these circumstances felt disingenuous. Sandwiched between the insights of Adrienne Rich and the challenge of the woman at the Existentialist Church, I knew I had some serious work to do. These seemingly small momentary silences are the stuff that give male hegemony its enormous power. I did not want to continue a life of lies, but what would substantive change entail for me? Learning the ugly truth about myself brought pain but also a certain relief at knowing myself better and being aware of the extent of my privilege more deeply. I would call on Adrienne Rich and the woman at the Existentialist Church for direction as I moved forward.

In the moment, change seemed daunting. Nonetheless, I pledged to myself that I would never knowingly 'leave the room'. In practice, this task has not been as difficult as I imagined it to be, and, in fact, I have found it to be quite liberating. Breaking silences that oppress others opened me to another source of peace and tranquility and put me in touch with my essential nature, rather than my socialized masculinity. As I observed my burgeoning change process, I also observed that breaking misogynistic silences brings a peace akin to that of meditative silences. Breaking one's silence is not so much an affront to other men as a call to excellence; a call for justice; and, a move toward the full expression of our humanity. And so, I would like to use *this* podium to encourage other men to take that same pledge and experience that same peace of mind. In my heart of hearts, I feel quite sure our collective shift away from these toxic silences can play a major role in ending male dominance.

Ghosts In The Blk Girl Throat
Khalisa Rae

The South will birth a new kind of haunting
in your black girl-ness, your black woman-ness.

Your body becomes a poached confection—
honeyed enigma pledging to be allegiant.
The muddied silk robe waving in their amber grains of
    bigotry.

Your skin—a rhetorical question, a
blood-stained equation no one wants to answer.

You will be the umber, tawny, terracotta
tongue spattered on their American flag,
beautiful brown-spangled anthem that we are.

You will be the bended knee in the boot of
their American Dream, and they will stitch your mouth
the color of patriarchy and call it black-girl magic
when you rip the seams.

Southern Belle is just another way to say:
stayed in her place on the right side of the pedestal.

Your sun-kissed skin will get caught in a crosshair
of questions like: *Where are you from?*
No, where are you really from?
You will be asked, *where are you from?*
more than you are asked, *how are you doing?*

Like this name, this tongue, this hair ain't
a tapestry of things they made you forget.
The continent they forced to the back of
your throat. And that's what they will come
for first – the throat.

They know that will be your super power,
your furnace of rebellion.

So they silence you before the coal burns.
Resurrecting monuments of ghosts on your street
to keep you from ever looking up.

Building a liquor store on every corner
so you don't notice the curated segregation.
They will call it 'redistricting'.

Muzzling the men with gallows for tongues
and calling it 'obedience school'.

Synthesizing our ghettos, graffiti-ing them in gold,
calling it 'urban development'.

They will make *bitch* a sweet exaggeration
of your name: *sit, speak, come*
when spoken to.

The leash will always be taut, always
gripping around a word you never said.

Ghosts In The Blk Girl Throat

Your body will be an apparition—
hologram of your former self.

Too much magic in one room—sorcery,
witch craft, and we will be witches, reassembling
the chandelier of our reflection.

We will spin a web of shade and make it a
place to rest under—broad oak that it is.

They will suck the mucus from your jubilation,
our gatherings now a cancer.

Clap back with shaking hands, 'cause that's all we've
got. This voice, this throat, this righteous indignation.

They start with the muzzle—always a taut muzzle to melt
the hard metallic of your wills. There will always be
a bit in the mouth of this horse that was too
stubborn to ever be spooked by ghosts.

"pink cookies in a plastic bag"[1]
stephen hicks

> "At a time when black males are losing ground on all fronts, and in many cases losing their lives, rather than creating a politics of resistance, many black males are simply acquiescing, playing the role of sexual minstrel. Exploiting mainstream racialized sexist stereotypes they go along to get along, feeling no rage that they must play the part of rapist or hypersexual stud to gain visibility."
>
> —bell hooks

PERHAPS, I'VE ACQUIESCED. Nah, let's be honest. I have played the hypersexual stud.

Usually, I would say something like, 'I'm not perfect'. Though it has a Captain Obvious ring to it, my use of the phrase has conveniently served as a feeble attempt at providing cover from accountability. By giving the pre-emptive 'I'm not perfect' sing-song, I hoped to silence critics, myself included. This strategy is used for the not-so-great things: if I'm running late, forgot to send an email, wasn't transparent in my intentions. 'I'm not perfect' is a defense mechanism when I failed to be deliberate. To be deliberate is to take responsibility for my actions—to be accountable. Accountability – that may be the reason why this convenient phrase is so utilized – accountability is scary. And yes, I remain scared of what accountability will dredge up. Stakes are high and the consequences can be steep. 'I'm not perfect' has, regrettably, been an underlying theme in much of my sexual dealings with women.

In the wake of the #MeToo stories flooding most of our social media timelines, I had a moment. A moment that I imagine most other straight, cis men experienced. Nervousness. Reluctance to engage. Apprehension. Steady streams of reactive thoughts rattling off simultaneously. Will someone tag me in one of their #MeToo posts? Will someone say I overstepped or violated their boundaries? I had empathy and was uncertain about what would be said. My kneejerk response morphed into self-preservation, taking deep breaths, hoping nobody said anything. Maybe an ex-girlfriend would describe my roll-over-loving strategy, which included sweet-talking clichés that now sound to me more like coercion than seeking enthusiastic consent. Maybe someone would come forward to say I didn't pick up on non-verbal cues before, during, and/or after sex. I thought of a couple incidents that I had already sought atonement for but that I still internally battled with my conscience to actually change my actions. #MeToo would potentially be a public reckoning.

#MeToo also had me thinking about the power of stories and whose voices have currency, and whose voices are often silenced. I saw in some massive way how toxic and harmful behaviors were affecting so many of my friends, partners, and colleagues. I took a moment and made a quick Facebook post, which read:

Re: #MeToo
i want to say sorry and express my apologies to
all who've been on the receiving end of my bs.
to be clear, my bs has been slut-shaming, body
shaming, unwanted advances, and womanizing.
i want to acknowledge my wrongdoing when
people shared with me their stories of experiencing various degrees of violation and i didn't
listen, or take their stories seriously, or didn't
fully hold the space for them. i am sorry. i am
sorry when i cracked rape jokes and gave the
benefit of the doubt when i suspected a friend of
doing foul stuff behind closed doors. i am sorry.
i am sorry for my misogyny and silencing. i am
sorry to my mans who i gave misguided advice
to when they asked about 'how to get women'.
i want to apologize to a specific woman from
college that i felt at the time should've given
me more affection/attention because i was a
'nice guy' doing nice things. i do not want to
continue this pattern and hope we are working toward creating a new normal—one with
healing, consent, and respect at the fore. peace
to all survivors.

The #MeToo movement has been immense and has inspired more mainstream conversations of toxic masculinity
and the social conditioning many boys and men have experienced and embodied. From my vantage point, most of the
mainstream conversations I've been a part of stop short of
nuance in the realm of toxic masculinity. We highlight the
extremes, which, as an unintended consequence, provides
cover for those who are engaged in toxic behaviors but are
considered 'nice guys', 'male feminists', or 'allies'. We readily
drag public figures on social media but haven't reconciled

our complicity or reckoned with our actions and inactions. Too often, the 'nice guy-bad boy' dichotomy has reigned supreme as the barometer for judging men—as if binaries perfectly encapsulate everyone's experience. I ask myself: where do I fall on this scale? And the question remains.

No 360° assessment has labeled me 'psychopath', and no friend or colleague has called me a 'sexist pig'—at least to my knowledge. I don't count any of the most contemporary villains (Trump, Cosby, Weinstein, R. Kelly) as heroes. However, if I move with full honesty, I return to my use of the 'I'm not perfect' cover to compensate for my refusal to grow in my dealings with women. This is complicity at best and... at worst. I sided with the nice guy template as window dressing but harbored patriarchal views on women, which deemed women as commodities or sex objects.

In college, I met a woman; we went on a few dates, and I quickly caught romantic feelings. She wasn't all that into me, but any attention from her meant everything to me. She asked me to help her with a project. I did. I had a hero complex. Weeks later, she received high praise for the final product. When she told me, I felt like the hero, but something was amiss. I reported all this back to a male friend, and he was annoyed on my behalf. That woman was at least supposed to give me some (translation: sex), he said. I didn't find the concept disgusting or preposterous. I thought he was spot-on. I was not going to approach her with that compensation arrangement. Let it happen it organically, I thought. It never happened. Instead, I stewed in resentment—the same resentment that had been boiling within me from my previous unrequited love days of high school. That couldn't be me. I was a nice guy. Plus, I had just finished reading *No Disrespect* from Sista Souljah. Nice guys don't have that kind of entitlement.

More than a decade removed from college, I think differently about the 'nice guy' construct. What distinguishes the nice guys from the bad boys may just be performance without substance. The performance of the nice guy (or male feminist) construct could include my use of charm school etiquette and Audre Lorde quotes. The nice guys – deep in their performance – need to be told and reminded that being nice or caring does not warrant access to anyone's body. No one owes me sex because I made a supposedly heartwarming gesture. I think society preaches and punishes the bad boys but assumes the best of the nice guy. And in the quiet, the nice guy is potentially violating people and using his good guy reputation to shield himself from accountability. This pattern silences his survivors.

If you knew better, you'd do better. Maybe, but I knew the standard was low, and I surfed above that bar, knowing I would not be held accountable. Little did I know that bar was so low that, in fact, I would be held in very high esteem within predominantly women, femme, and LGBTQ spaces.

I imagine I've been considered 'good enough' to sit at their lunch tables or 'the best of the worst' in terms of my cis, straight, maleness. Picture me as the overachieving nice guy. I didn't use the canon of derogatory terms for women or LGBTQ. I didn't crack rape jokes and didn't laugh out loud when I heard them. I spoke of advocating for transgender women. I would name-drop Fannie Lou Hamer or Marsha P. Johnson when convenient. I would speak of intersectionality and practice amplification during staff meetings, which would look like me reiterating what one of my female colleagues' statements and giving them credit for their idea suggestion.

I sidelined my Wall Street corporate pursuits for social justice and public health work. As my career ascended, I found myself in more spaces where I was the anomaly: the cool, straight, cis, black guy with muscles, a beard, and a master's degree. Grandstanding and performing were my key go-to moves. And being in those spaces long enough, I eased into behaviors and practices that did not fully recognize people (specifically women) as more than conduits of my pleasure. It wasn't benevolent patriarchy; more like a woke misogynist with great polish. A nice guy engaging in the same toxicity as his supposed evil contemporaries but with a softer charm.

#MeToo has named many, but not all, culprits. #MeToo has me thinking of all of the violations perpetuated by the nice guys—the social justice guys who cite Rebecca Solnit in one breath and who actively silence and control people in the next. Me.

I hurt lots of people on the way here to 32 years old. I diminished people's feelings and prioritized detachment. Using the colloquialism, I thought with my other head. I used women for my pleasures and maintained imbalanced relationships with them. I was sex-positive without fully recognizing/affirming/celebrating the people I was having sex with.

"Shorty, let me tell you about my only vice."[2]

I quietly rationalized my sexual pursuits as making up for lost time. I was a late bloomer. My schoolmates in middle and high school and college held hands, made out by the lockers, planned mall adventures, talked on the phones for hours, met parents, took prom photos, experimented with sex, and covered all the bases. Not me. I sat lonesome. Never, not once, did I experience that intimate connection with someone else throughout high school and college. Secretly, I was building a wall of resentment toward women, brick by brick. I said to myself, once I get the ladies, I ain't slowing down.

During my college years, I wished for what some would deem 'the good kind of problems'—those rooted mostly in excess. I wanted to be turning down and saying 'no' to multitudes of women interested in me. And in a whisk of years, I crossed the attractive threshold, people reacted a bit differently to me—fewer women flaked out on dates; fewer women gave me fake phone numbers; more women inquired about my evening and weekend plans. My time had come. I began doing my thing, all with little regard. This was a time when a friend called me 'a walking dick'.

"I was ex-girl to next girl."[3]

I was 25 years old, and had a few things going for me. I saw women as sexual conquests to be recorded in my files. I made very little effort to transform my perception of women into a full engagement of who they were complete with thoughts, opinions, beliefs, and experiences. Nah, that was too much. What mattered most was my presentation and sealing the deal—bonus points if neither party gained emotional attachment. I placed more energy in my sexual performance than in fostering intimacy. It worked best (for me) if we kept things transactional. My performance superseded my substance.

I strengthened a skillset through these transactional dealings with women—a polished approach, a detachment. I used sex as a mechanism to validate my worth. I relied on sex to substitute for meaningful interpersonal connections.

I wallowed in guilt in the months preceding #MeToo's peak. In the evening hours of Friday, November 11, 2016, I finally did something. In an attempt to strike reconciliation or some semblance of it, I reached out to almost all of the women I could think of were often treated like a booty call or a 'jump-off' only to boost my fragile ego. I sat in a dim-ly-lit basement apartment thumbing away text messages. I must have texted 30 women that night—women who trusted me enough with physical intimacy and to whom I responded with coy tactics, lackluster affection, and conversation about everything except my feelings and intentions. I imagined this communication mode would be more conducive for naming my misdeeds and not expecting an immediate response:

- Hey ___, I don't think I made this clear but I'm sorry if I ever shortchanged you in any way. You are special and I didn't come correct and value you when we shared time together. I'm glad you are doing super. I am wishing you well in everything you touch or get involved with. Please continue to take good care of yourself.
- Hello. I want to apologize for whatever hurt I caused you. I am sorry for not being forthcoming with you. I also apologize for any inauthenticity. I'm honored ___ saw fit for us to meet. I hope you are doing well and you are thriving.
- ___, kinda random but I want to reach out to you and say hi. I also want to say sorry for any wrongdoing or anything I did to hurt you in any way years ago. I am glad to see you doing well. I am wishing you much success in all things. I'm glad that you and I shared time together and I'm grateful that you are here in the world.

I do not want to send those types of text messages again. The hurt doesn't need to continue to a new group of women.

I travel with my regrets and remorse, for it didn't have to be this way. I'm keenly aware when author Carmen Maria Machado writes, "how easily we accept women's pain as collateral damage in men's self-discovery." Several women were on the receiving end of my unresolved traumas, and I didn't do them any favors in extending my toxicity

Within the last year, I joined a group of people deliberately addressing toxic masculinity in Washington, DC. They have a program aimed at equipping masculine-identifying persons with tools for emotional labor, consent, and bystander intervention. The program isn't a magical pill;

however, for me, they planted some seeds in fertile soil. I began to unpack the motivations behind being so reckless in my dealings with women. I began to recognize the toxicity of my actions within the context of masculinity. Within that space, I finally aired how I used sex as a tool to validate my self-worth, so I would not have to exert more of myself. I could hide behind a false self instead of bringing my authentic self to my relationships with women.

Writing this essay while knowing my past feels bizarre. This may be my imposter syndrome once again. Thinking back to those behaviors that led to that November night of text messages, I want to honor those women and not lead more men astray.

We know there are many forms of performance—be it through gender, sexuality, self-promotion, or anything else. To be 'cool' or 'woke' is performative as well. I'm exhausted of performing—namely, I'm exhausted of grandstanding as the nice guy who uses the mask of his perceived distance from toxic masculinity, patriarchy, and rape culture to avoid doing any personal work.

Yes, I have strong opinions about what's going on in the world. Yes, I think we can harness healthier masculinities. Yes, I can make a change, but I want to do it from an authentic space. I want to be less concerned with convincing women that I'm a good catch. Performative wokeness, I've learned, has a hey-look-at-me quality. More emphasis is placed on receiving brownie points than actually making a point. The sure-fire way for me to gauge if I am performing is based on my willingness to be in meaningful connection: *Am I aiming to connect with this person or show them that I am a good person?*

My text messages were meant to remove the sheen and move myself toward accountability. I want to make space for those who have been silenced to express themselves. I have to be careful because I recognize even my accountability-seeking efforts could become performative. It's not meant to be an act coming from a self-serving, oblivious space. I am trying my best to translate my thoughts and feelings into meaningful change. I now know that there will be some sort of reckoning for my actions—good, bad, or without description. My actions have to speak louder than my words. In doing so, I am actively self-defining, healing, and resisting—not merely acquiescing.

Soundtrack for reading:
1. LL Cool J "Pink Cookies in a Plastic Bag (Remix)"
2. A Tribe Called Quest "Electric Relaxation"
3. Gang Starr "Ex Girl to Next Girl"
4. Wordsworth "Trust"
5. Jean Carne "Don't Let It Go to Your Head"

College Dreams
Steven Strafford

PERHAPS YOU KNOW a musical-theatre-loving gay man. Perhaps you are one. If you don't happen to know a musical-theatre-loving gay man, I want you to understand how very exciting it would have been to this musical-the-atre-loving gay man to receive an invitation to see the original Broadway revival cast of the musical *Chicago*. If you are a sports fan, imagine your favorite team playing in a heretofore unheard-of playoff game. If you are a music fan, that singer is giving a living room performance, and you are invited. It was the summer of 1997. My college professor, Dave (not his name) invited me to see *Chicago* on Broadway. I was *thrilled.*

It was the summer between my sophomore and junior years. I had spent the summer living with two girlfriends in a double room, sleeping on a couch. I was waiting tables at an Italian restaurant, and I had brought my beer pong game up to a level of competitiveness that had me passing out in front of the dorm where we were playing. I was young. I was in college. I was a burgeoning alcoholic. The world was mine. I was having a summer of fun. So, when I got an invitation to go into the city to see a recently much-heralded revival of a Kander and Ebb musical, I leapt at the chance.

Dave was an acting professor at my college. He was much beloved and respected by the students; we knew his wife, Molly, who seemed great with her dry sense of humor, and his tremendously adorable daughter, Melissa (not their names). He had given me a few opportunities to prove myself in productions he directed. I felt seen by him. He was exhaustive and exhausting in his notes on my work, but I was young and hungry to learn how to be a better actor. I took each note without question. (A quality as an actor, I should learn to revisit, but that's a story for another day.) We were taught to be sponges. We should wring ourselves out of old habits. He would be providing the way forward. He would be building us from the ground up. I felt like he was my mentor.

I remember how hard I was trying not to smoke ciga-rettes as we were walking around the city. By the summer between my junior and senior years of college, I was easily a pack a day smoker. I remember really wanting to smoke, but I didn't want to be seen as a smoker especially because I had been in a musical he had directed earlier in the year. I wanted to be seen as an adult who smoked, but didn't need to smoke—someone who chose to smoke because it delight-ed them and made them feel worldly. Basically, I wanted to seem like a 1940's movie star, not a working-class kid who smoked the same cigarettes his mom did. I wanted so desper-ately to please this man who had taken interest in me and my training. I wanted to be the ideal student for him. I didn't want my bad habits to somehow make him think less of me. I gargled with Listerine and obsessively washed my hands hoping to hide any traces of smoke from my person.

We talked a lot that day about my future. He told me I was talented. He said I had the abilities to act if I wanted to, but I needed to pull myself together a bit. Less smoking (What? Me?), drinking (Had I not been better at hiding it?), smoking pot, etc. Basically, it was a wake-up call from a mentor wrapped up in a trip to see Bebe Neuwirth belt her face off. I must say, it was effective. I felt put in my place. I would no longer do things that made me less than the best in his eyes. I would be better. I would do better. He would see it. He would be proud. Then, we saw the show. It was amazing. I wanted a life in the theatre. I wanted to be as good as those people up there. I thought to myself, maybe I could do it if I listened to him and pulled myself together.

The trip home was uneventful. The usual breakdown of the show we just saw occurred. Dave told me all about the original production and how people didn't appreciate the show. I went on and on about how I didn't realize that a character in drag was a man. I was shocked! (This is one of the moments that charms present day me about yesteryear me. I was so delightfully naïve.) We talked about how great the dancing was. We laughed. I felt really, really good. I felt part of something older than me. He talked about the big project he wanted to direct in the coming year, and how I should be the lead in it. I felt like I was at the beginning of my future. One more year of college, during which this man would help me become the actor I wanted to be, followed by a life in the city!

We got back to the college campus, and everything seemed so quaint and woodsy. We had just been in New York City seeing the most cynical of all musicals. To be back in this liberal arts enclave in the forest felt like going back in time to the present. We stood outside the dorm I was staying in at the time, and we talked some more about the show. If you'll allow me this indulgence, I would like to write the next part of this essay as a play. I write plays. It's how I best write conversations. I mean, what are you going to do, say no? Well, I guess you could skip this next section as a form of saying no… I am losing the thread. Okay. So, we're standing outside the dorm. I have replayed this conversation so many times over in my head to see if it meant what I thought it meant—what I think it means:

(Lights up on a woodsy dorm quad.
A professor, in his late forties and student who
is 20 years old finish laughing about
a musical theatre joke.)

DAVE
So. What are you doing now?

STEVEN
Oh.

(STEVEN pauses. It is late. And although
the day has been great, he is unsure of what
he and his professor would go do at midnight.
He will probably go find people who are
drinking or smoking pot as he is a burgeoning
alcoholic and drug addict, but he wants to act
like he's heard his professor's words of
advice, so he says:)

I'm just going to bed, I think. I have work tomorrow, and I should get some sleep. Thanks so much for the tickets.

(Here is a long pause. The sort of pause where
one can feel like maybe they said
something wrong)

DAVE
Oh. I just thought we could get a drink. This was a great night.

(If this were a movie this would be a great place for the sky to go all fast and the color to drain from the woods.)

STEVEN

Yeah. It was. I just need to go to bed.

DAVE

(laughing) C'mon. I know you're going to have at least a drink tonight...

(STEVEN laughs, but it's an empty sound based on the fact that DAVE has spent the day saying that STEVEN drinks too much and needs to change that, but now DAVE seems to be using this information to prolong an awkward ending to a very nice day.)

STEVEN

Well, not tonight, I guess.

(At this point, DAVE's face changes. It's difficult to say what exactly happens except to say that what once seemed supportive and flirtatious, now looks twisted about. DAVE's face suggests someone at once wounded and looking to wound.)

STEVEN (cont'd)

(said in one breath) Thanks again for the tickets. Really. It was so nice of you. Please say hi to Molly and Melissa! Night!

(STEVEN runs inside. He finds friends. He drinks and smokes all of the cigarettes. He runs

these few moments over and over in his head.
Did that just happen? He will do this for a long
time after this play ends.)

LIGHTS DOWN. END OF PLAY.

If he were hot, if he looked like an elbow-patch wearing, JCrew model of a professor, I probably would have invited him back to see if something could happen. But, as it was, he was not. He was not a physically attractive man. I didn't want anything to happen physically with this man. Despite my shock, I knew what this moment was, and I wasn't interested. I did not want to acknowledge it for what it was, and I wanted to shut it down as fast as possible.

And that was that. An awkward moment that could easily be refuted. He had not said anything that couldn't be denied, but in the air between us, what had transpired, what had been offered would always sit. It was a moment both cloudy and clear because I knew it. I knew he knew it. I knew he knew I knew it. And it could never be proven. It was private. It was a man in authority and me. It would be replayed over and over in my head. I would think, "Perhaps, I looked too much into it. Maybe this married man was just interested in hanging out longer. Maybe he just wanted to have a drink and maybe smoke some pot with a guy who was sure to have a line on that stuff? Maybe he wanted to just spend a few more moments telling me what was up with my future? Maybe he just hadn't had the chance to discuss Ann Reinking's comedic chops?" I spent many moments knowing that it had happened while at the very same moment doubting that it happened. To know something while constantly questioning your own knowing is the basis of some serious self-gaslighting.

I do know what happened weeks later in his acting class in the fall because that happened in public.

Things, come the fall, felt different with Dave. I was no longer the one to whom he made the jokey reference. I was ignored in class and generally dismissed outright. I felt left out in the cold. For our first round of scenes given in his advanced acting class, I was given the role of Demetrius in *A Midsummer Night's Dream*. After a few weeks of rehearsal with my very talented scene partner (Hey, Kristen! I'm using your real name!), our turn to present to the class arrived. We began performing the scene. We were getting tons of laughs. All in all, it felt like a success.

We waited for notes from our professor. After a few (deserved) compliments for Kristen, Dave looked at me. "Steven," he said with a deep sigh, "It's just... your voice. Every single word you say, it sounds like not quite a man speaking. Unless you get serious vocal training, and I mean serious training, I just feel like all you'll ever do... all you could do is play homosexuals or aliens." He laughed, and then said, "I'd like to see the scene again, but I just don't think I can hear you do this again. Acting isn't for everyone in the end. Sit down."

The moments after these words were in a deep vacuum of noise and feeling. I shut it all down. I heard what I can only assume were the words I was supposed to hear: *You're too gay to go be an actor of any real note or acclaim. Give up. Do something else. Sit down.*

Looking back on this moment now, he had all the power. He always did. Every single step of the way was his to run. The only power I had was in saying no. And I did. It upended him in a way. I feel strange making a ton of conjecture about his internal feelings towards me. It feels unfair of me as a writer of this essay. However, I have thought a lot about it. I guess what I'm left with are questions. Was he merely exacting revenge? Was my rejection one of a long list of rejections, and I merely represented men who weren't interested in him sexually? Was my very gayness, my voice, my mannerisms, my living openly and freely as who I am, was that what offended him? Was he actually trying to help? Was he really worried for my future? Did he think being gay would truly be a handicap? Was it just a need to silence me? Was he just reminding me who was in charge?

I don't get to know the answer to these. I am mad that I have spent so many hours of my life since then asking myself about this event, his motivations, my actions, and what could have been different. How many hours were lost to the hashing and rehashing of this event? What could I have done? What could I have written? What could I have pursued? What Netflix series could I have finished?

After he shamed me in class, I didn't tell anyone about what precipitated these remarks. I did what he said. I followed his instructions. I sat down. I withdrew into myself until next semester. I disappeared.

Thankfully, my friends, this story has a (reasonably) happy ending. The next semester my small liberal arts college invited a playwright and actress to come in and teach an advanced acting class. This woman, Leslie, would reorient me back towards a path I am still on today.

She and I were walking on a path across campus after class one day, and she asked about my need to code switch. Code switching, in my particular case, is trying to pass for straight, changing my voice and my mannerisms to act like the sort of man Dave had told me I should aspire to be. It's a practice that I wish I never did at all. I wish I always stayed in the pocket of being completely honest in my voice and body. These days, I mainly code switch with delivery guys or people who come to my home for repairs. I'm always disappointed with myself when I do it. I drop my voice. I puff up my chest. I relax my jaw until I breathe a bit with my mouth.

I hate that I do it. It is instinctive and self-protecting. Dave is not the only person who taught me to do it. It is something that everyday culture in a heteronormative world has taught me. It is hard to unlearn.

So, I was walking along with my new acting professor, when she asked about why I was so concerned with the need to butch it up in class. She was confused. She said that although she had known I was gay, she didn't feel it affected my work when playing straight characters. She pressed me as to why I thought this was the case. I told her the whole story. It came out faster than words should ever travel out of a mouth. She listened. At the end of the story, she stopped. She took a deep breath. She looked up at the sky. She looked back at me. She said, "Honey. That man is in the closet. That man is jealous of your comfort with yourself. That man tried to make you feel as bad as he feels. As for acting, you'll play a million different things depending on who is casting the show! AND. If you ONLY played homosexuals and aliens in your whole career, do you know what you would have? A CAREER." She laughed and said, "Steven, you are going to be just fine."

Although it wasn't a complete in-the-moment reversal, it was the beginning of a change. I would, over the course of many years as a professional actor, come to terms with exactly who I am and how I'm seen. I would figure out that it is important for me to be myself entirely in life, so I can pretend to be other people on stage.

Sexual harassment and the abuse of power is an insidious and long-term, damaging thing. I think of the 20-year-old kid, a mess who needed guidance and found it, only for it to be turned upside down. I get sad for him. It's confusing when the person who treated you in such a troubling way is revered by others as a great guy. It will never not be confusing. It will always be a place in time where I worry, "Was I being too sensitive? Did I misunderstand? Is this even worth writing about?" When I take time to reflect and treat myself with the compassion and care I would give anyone else, I know that I was not being too sensitive. I did understand. A man with power and authority over me implied we could have a sexual encounter. When I denied him, he withdrew and ultimately shamed me for being gay in front of my peers. It was wrong. So, I am writing about it. I am showing up with every last bit of my very gay voice.

Faking It
Alandra Markman

I MUST HAVE LEFT SCHOOL, gone home and slept, and come back, I usually think to myself. I feel rested. I am dressed in different clothing. Time has passed since yesterday afternoon, and now it's the morning again. My first period class is starting soon. I feel vaguely embarrassed that I don't remember anything about what happened after I went home. I can't bring to mind any of the details, like if I stopped anywhere after school, or what I had for dinner. Often very little of my homework is done, but I can't say what I did instead. The papers in my bookbag are in the same random order that I stuffed them in yesterday. I'm not sure if I've done all my reading. I feel unprepared for everything.

In drama club, we sometimes discuss the 'actor's nightmare': being thrown on stage into a play you have not studied or even read. You have no context for what you are doing. You don't know who your character is or what any of your lines are supposed to be. All the other actors have rehearsed their parts well, and you have to keep pace with them, speaking into the gaps they leave for you. Whatever you think up has to make some kind of sense or you'll be booted out of the theater by the stage manager. I watch a thrill of fright pass through the class as they contemplate this scenario, followed by relief as they realize it's only a fantasy. I don't feel like I can join in either the fright or the relief, though. It's too real to me.

So while the others are talking about it, I often flash on another theater memory: my mother taking me to see the musical *Les Misérables* live on Broadway. In one of the first scenes, the street whores of Paris sing about their sorry lot in life. For some reason I can't fathom, this scene feels intensely personal for me. Even on the second or third time seeing it, my cheeks explode with heat and I break out into a cold sweat. My legs start trembling and I start praying for the song to end. I look over at my mother, who is also transfixed in a way I rarely see her, muttering dark curses under her breath or batting away a tear. During other parts of the musical, she jokes or whispers things to me, but during this one scene she never makes eye contact. She won't even turn her head.

The word 'prostitute' is never spoken in my household. More modern terms like 'escort' or 'sex worker' are off limits too. When my mother dresses up to go meet one of her clients (whom I've privately called the 'bad men' since I was little), and I ask where she's going, all she says is 'out'. With that one word, she shuts the door, and I am home alone for several hours at least. I wonder what she expects me to believe about her obvious lies and omissions, but I never dwell on it for long. Those are good nights for me. My awful memory clears up a little. There's usually a TV dinner in the freezer for me to defrost. I can play all the computer games I want. I might even get some homework done.

I have to be extra careful if she comes back late at night or early in the morning, though, because she's always in a bad mood. She roars hateful things at herself, and at me if I happen to be in the same room. If she sees me, she stops. For a moment I don't know if she's going to throw something at me or grab me and hold me as tight as she can. The latter is usually worse. She pulls me into her bedroom, sets me down on her mattress on the floor, throws off her fur coat and high-heeled shoes. Then off come her sheer shirt and lingerie. Her face is a dense mask of smeared makeup contorted with rage and she smells like vodka and too much perfume.

I don't know how to say what happens next. I can't describe it clearly, but I know it involves her getting naked and me being too terrified to do anything. I try to make out what she's saying, though I feel I'm a great distance away. She tells me to put things inside of her: metal studs, black rubber cones, my hands. Often I am too far outside of my body to be able to move, so she simply grabs my hand and moves it inside her. I am only a tool. She smells like rotting fish and stress and moans like a wounded animal for an unbearably long time. I feel my mind grasping for anything it can reach: math problems, song lyrics, high scores. Eventually it gives up, and I find myself falling asleep. I wake up later in my own room, and my alarm is going off again. It's time to go back to school.

My first period class is Chorus, and the voice teacher, Ms. D, is exquisitely beautiful. I often spend the whole class absorbed in watching her lips move and her breasts sway as she conducts, hardly caring whether I'm hitting my notes or not. Sometimes I even let myself feel melty inside, but that leads quickly into sharp pains and confusion and things I don't want to be thinking about. At least I can allow myself some jealousy of her pianist boyfriend Mr. G, who comes in sometimes to accompany us. The class gossips a lot about them. I tune out and picture myself up there with my guitar alone with Ms. D, playing a flawless duet before she leans in for a kiss.

I don't think I could ever have a real girlfriend, but I have friends, supposedly. Other kids ask how I am, what's happening. I never know what to say other than 'nothing', 'all right', 'okay'. I feel like a fake. Everybody else seems to have changing moods, ready answers, but I look like an automaton, only ever experiencing one thing. I'd be too ashamed to admit I don't know how I am, or even who I am. When I try to tune into my deeper feelings, I almost always get rage, a blood-boiling rage bigger than any person could ever deal with. All I can do is ignore it. It's too intense to talk to anybody about, too intense for school. Other people mainly seem to experience mild emotions like 'disappointment' or 'excitement'. I do my best to stay within that range. After all, I don't believe I have any rational reason to feel so upset all the time. None that I can always remember, anyway. None that feel *solid*, none that I'm absolutely sure of.

I've also been strictly ordered to trust no one except my mother, so I do my best not to open up to anyone else. It's especially important to avoid any extended conversation with adults who see me often, like teachers and counselors. My mother had taught me the phrase 'mandated reporter' by the time I was five years old, meaning those who are legally-obligated to report suspicions of child abuse. She says they could get me taken away to a foster home, where I'd have no family and no one to care about me at all. It's better to hide bruises like I hide my rage. The same small tricks and calculated silences that hide me from my friend's questions usually work for their parents too. The parents are too polite to ask me why I'm so often at their houses but never give an invitation to my house. My mother, as usual, says nothing about our real reasons. She tells me I can't have people over because our house is too small and dirty, that my more well-off friends would judge me and stop wanting to hang out with me if they ever came over. I half-believe her.

I'm dimly aware that I have my own private theory as well. I figure if there were something really wrong happening, my mother wouldn't be responsible for it. She's very sick, but I know that deep down she loves me. She must believe that I'm doing something wrong and that by punishing me she'll be able to correct it. I came up with this idea when I was very small, before I could even talk, but I still think it might be true. There's probably something bad about how I act or even how I think, and that means I deserve anything I get. If I could learn to be better or more obedient, it would all stop. My mother would stop grabbing me and pulling me into her room. She'd stop inviting the bad men to our house; maybe she'd even stop going out to see them. Neither she nor the men would ever touch me again.

I stay at school as long as I can. We're done at 3:30, but I'm often there till 5:00 or 6:00 in the evening, learning parts with the drama club, editing the literary magazine, journaling in the computer lab. The one place I feel at home is with the improv comedy troupe. At least there, we're *all* faking it, not just me. The security guards are used to seeing me as the last student out of the building. I can't tell them why I choose to stay so long. Even I don't really know why, but I can feel my chest tighten and my head swim with nausea when I think about going home. Shooting pains I'm barely aware of during the day start flaring up; I have trouble drawing a deep breath. I know she's there, and maybe some of the bad men are there too.

Whenever I catch my first glimpse of the bad men at our house, I can already feel myself starting to fall asleep. Something in my mind knows how to make this happen. They are here in my house again, it says, and I don't want to be here for this. One minute I'm wide awake, and the next I'm completely out. Sometimes I sleep the whole night through and wake up the next day. Sometimes I'm back within a few hours, waking up suddenly in the middle of the night. I have no memory of how I got from fully dressed at the door to naked in my bed, and I wonder how it happened. Often I feel a dull aching pain in my butt and lower back, or there's a weird taste in my mouth and nose like ammonia. There are sometimes lines or bruises on my legs and arms. I get up and brush my teeth. Then I feel like I have to poop but I can't; only a little bit of air or a trickle of goopy water comes out. I shrug it off and go back to sleep.

Sometimes, instead of waking up, I have a recurring dream. I dream that I'm waking up because of noises from the kitchen. It sounds like a party is going on. I get up, walk down the hallway from my room, and there on the throw rug are giant muppet-like creatures, birds and furry animals, dancing and chanting. It's terrifyingly surreal, but I'm usually curious enough to get myself to stay and watch them for a while, or even to dance with them. This dream has been with me since I was little, and it feels like it stands for something else, something I can almost put my finger on. Maybe it's that I am going to dance and sing no matter what happens to me. Maybe it's that I will always have at least a few friends who understand me without my having to use words. It could even be that the bad men too are part of a larger dance, where roles like man and whore come and go.

All I know is that, tired or not, with memories or without, I am going back out tomorrow. I am not going to give up on this hollow life. I am not going to kill myself, like I've often thought about doing. When I'm alone in the kitchen in the mornings, my mother still asleep after an outcall, I'll sometimes hold out a butcher knife with both hands and wonder what it would feel like to plunge it into my chest. My body hates the idea. My body grows bigger and stronger every day, and its voice grows clearer and deeper. It often repeats the message that has kept me sane but also silent all these years: try to forget your pain and remember your pleasure. It always tells me to put the knife down, take a deep breath, and focus on pouring myself a bowl of sugary cereal.

The sugar gives me a small high and feels good. I can't say there's no sweetness in my life. One time I almost realized my dream of a duet with Ms. D. I was headed to an improv troupe meeting on the top floor of my school when I happened to wind up alone with her in the elevator. I'd been softly singing "I Am The Walrus" to myself when she stepped in on the second floor. She recognized it and sang a few bars with me as we shared this fleeting privacy. I thought I was going to faint when I heard her voice so close to mine like that, our song filling the tiny space. When I think about the goosebumps I had on my arms, I can't go through with hurting myself. No matter how much pain I'm in now, I have to stay alive and keep up a facade of wellness if there are going to be more moments like that. I am going to improvise all the way to graduation, if only because I want to see what comes next.

Listening To My Body
Nadia Colburn

ONE DAY, IN MY MID-THIRTIES, I woke up from a nap and remembered.

At almost the exact same moment, I found myself at a silence so great it was physical.

I could not speak. I could not even breathe. Instead, my body began to shake.

The silence – the horror – was suffocating.

And the only way I could exhale was through a scream.

Thank goodness Eric was next door in the park with the kids; I didn't want to scare them. *What was happening?*

Panic attacks such as this had happened to me before as a younger woman—these experiences in which I shook, unable to breathe and then could breathe again only through a scream. But in my early twenties, there had been no thought, no memory, no fear attached to these events—at least none that I could recognize.

This was different. I felt utter terror at this feeling that I was at the same time remembering and completely unable to remember.

Very gradually, I put language to that memory, and over many years, through therapy, through writing, through the gentle patience and support of Eric, through yoga, through meditation and spiritual practice, I pieced together the story.

I was sexually assaulted when I was very young, in bed, by a babysitter. Eventually, my mother helped me fill in the details. It took a long time to get there, and by the time my mother and I could have a conversation about what had happened, I had already done a lot of healing in the dark on my own.

But to focus on what happened in the assault is to get my story wrong.

My story is the story of the silence of not knowing.

It is the story of learning to listen to what could not be spoken in words or thoughts and of coming to name the unspeakable.

It is the story of the cost of that experience. And also, finally, the gift of it.

NOW I HAVE LEARNED that when something is too difficult to process, the mind and the body split. It is a protective measure. And when there is no narrative, especially when there are no reliable witnesses and when the experience occurs when a child is very young, the memory can become cut off, stored in a part of the brain inaccessible to language.

Even if the mind does not consciously know what has happened, the body has been imprinted. It holds a physical, cellular memory. The trauma is set into the nervous system. As Bessel Van der Kolk says, it is the body that 'keeps the score'.

This is my experience. From the time that I was very young, I was drawn to the places language could not go. Those silent places had a magical allure.

If there was sometimes a gentle magical wonder in silence, there was also a dangerous, shadowy magnetic pull to those silences.

In college, I was drawn to the poetry of W. H. Auden. His early poetry is full of language and landscapes cut off from themselves, of secret impenetrable codes, of slippages of meanings, and of deep pathways that seem to lead beyond language.

I called my undergraduate thesis "This Land Cut Off Will Not Communicate".

In Auden's poetry, the land is also often the body. And though Auden, who wrote as a gay man in a time in which to be gay was to break the law, put words to what Lord Alfred Douglas called "love that dare not speak its name," his poems, I argued, were not just trying to express that love. They were, I suggested, trying to express the inexpressible itself.

I myself did not know what I meant by that idea, and I could not quite explain it to others. I did not know then that I was also talking about the inexpressible I carried within myself.

At 22, I was searching for something in that thesis that I didn't have the tools yet to recognize or articulate personally.

It left me feeling personally frustrated.

A few months after I graduated, my body broke down.

This is when I started to have what I called 'attacks'.

The first time it happened, I was lying in bed (perhaps not a coincidence). I couldn't sleep. And suddenly, I couldn't breathe. I felt I was being suffocated, and then instead of breath, only a long drawn out scream came out of my mouth.

My mind searched for answers.

I went to the hospital. But the doctors could find nothing wrong with me.

Over the next month, these 'attacks' became more and more frequent, so frequent that instead of moving to Paris with Eric, we both decided to move back to my parents' home to New York City where I could visit more doctors.

Doctor after doctor had a different theory: I had hypoglycemic attacks; I had a tumor on my pancreas; I had a faulty endocrine system.

But test after test came back normal.

Only after all the tests came back normal did the doctors say — it was the same every time — you must be having panic attacks. Then they'd get up, show me to the door, and close it behind me.

The doctors never suggested that I get treatment for panic attacks. Instead they seemed to be implying that I was just a crazy young woman who had been wasting their time and they'd had enough of me.

This, of course, was its own form of silencing.

I tried a few therapists and eventually started to go to one weekly, but I didn't find the sessions particularly helpful and they didn't help me get to any new insights.

If my body was speaking to me, I didn't know how to listen. And apparently the people around me didn't have the tools to help me either.

So instead of listening more carefully to my body, I felt that my body was betraying me, getting in the way of the full, happy, life I wanted to be living. I made it my job to learn to navigate around my body's betrayals and get on with my life.

I changed my diet: I took all sugar and gluten out; I ate lots of vegetables and protein. I learned to anticipate when an attack might be coming on, and I managed.

Eric and I did eventually go to Paris. We came back and I started graduate school. My life was rich and full, but I lived with a near-constant background hum of anxiety, a sense that I was living under a shadow; the inner and the outer world both seemed too much for me at times, and I never knew when my body might suddenly break down.

Periodically, I tried different doctors.

Finally, four years after I'd first gotten sick, both Eric and I were diagnosed with an amoebic parasite.

Presumably, we had picked it up in Mexico, where we'd gotten sick from bad water two years earlier; the parasites had slowly grown within us and then had gotten out of control.

After a round of powerful antibiotics, Eric's digestive issue that had bothered him (but that he'd pretty much ignored) got much better. And I stopped having my 'attacks'.

I thought that was the end of the story.

I got pregnant with Gabriel at the end of the summer. I was ready to embrace my good health.

But the story, of course, wasn't over.

Every few years, I'd have another attack. I'd go back to the doctor to get more antibiotics.

I went on with my life, moved forward, and had another child.

Eventually, I began to listen to my body differently. It wanted me to slow down. I did.

I had been writing poetry, but I began writing prose and started to piece together narratives.

I found an attentive therapist who made me feel heard and gave me tools to listen to myself more fully. I developed a mindfulness practice. I read and I grew.

Many years passed.

And then I woke up from that nap. That day, I remembered something that I did not have language for. And my body, in reaction to that memory, went into panic.

It was literally my awakening. A waking up to what I did not want to know. To my own silences. To what, in that silence, I had somehow always known.

OVER THE NEXT YEARS, I engaged in very intense healing. This is the easy way to say it. It means, however, that I came into contact with great pain and horror that at times threatened to upend my life and myself.

To stay with the memory of a traumatic event, to actually pay attention to it was clearly what I needed to do, but doing so was like holding my whole body and psyche and soul out over an electric shock wave and just staying there in the intensity and horror.

Mindfulness practices helped me not get trapped in that shock, helped me come back to the present and be available also for the joy and wonder of my life, for my kids and my family. It was also my mindfulness practice that helped me stay with what was within me, not run away, and begin to put shape and name to the memories that I was having.

It was only when I stopped fighting the images and scenes that I was recalling, only when I started to accept them, that my nervous system calmed down.

And it was only by going into the silence, listening, and slowly naming what I was experiencing, that I healed.

This was very, very hard. I did not want to see what was there for me to see. I did not want to name it.

Writing helped. In part, writing helped because it gave me language in a safe space, without needing to worry that anyone would hear or judge. At first, I wrote only in a completely locked part of my computer. I wrote in fragments and didn't re-read.

Then I slowly pieced together sentences that I shared with Eric and my therapist. Speaking was at times all but impossible. At first, I could only say *something unbearable happened to me*. I would need to stop to catch my breath. I felt as if I was engaged in an internal battle: the part of me that wanted to speak was struggling against the part of me that wanted to remain silent.

In my childhood, as my parents' firstborn, I played the role of the perfect, innocent, pure child. To admit back then that something had happened to me would have shattered that image I so treasured.

It would also have shattered the image of our family, the perfect family where nothing could go wrong.

This dynamic of silence – of not talking about the problems that were in our family – was not unique to my trauma. We didn't talk about my father's rages or my mother's temper. We didn't talk about the ways in which we were angry with or unhappy with each other or with ourselves. We were a perfect unit. If the outer world was a dangerous place, our home was the perfect haven where nothing could go wrong. And later, when my father had an affair, we didn't speak of that either.

The code of perfection in my family was so strong that I must have felt that it could cover up anything terrible. The assault had almost killed me—or that, at least, was my experience of being held down and suffocated. I did not think I would live through it.

To break my silence would have been to go back to that space of utter horror where the whole world fell apart, where nothing could keep any one of us safe, where we were all utterly alone.

And so as a child, silence, not speaking about certain things, was the safer option. It was my family's protection, just as, in that moment of the assault, splitting from my body had been a protective measure.

In my family's silence was also our love. In our silence was also our identity.

And so in speaking what had happened, I was unsettling a deep, deep pattern of who I was, of who my whole family was. Even if my adult self was strong and bold enough to do this, that child self was still in me, still terrified of what might happen if I spoke the whole truth.

The truth had the danger of breaking apart not only my external world, but also the internal world that was still on some level of my own making.

So many children, in order to keep their world safe, in order to believe that their parents are keeping them safe, assume self-blame. In my child mind, there was something wrong with me for this terrible, disgusting, painful act to have happened. I had a deep rooted shame in believing that I was not the pure, untouched girl that I was supposed to be.

Only gradually could I get over the shame of being abused by telling others, first only my best, most-trusted friends—and then women in a support group. Only when I had really deeply healed could I tell others about what had happened and write about it publicly.

To recover, we need to be able to put our experiences into language that communicates what has happened, and we need to be heard—by ourselves and by others.

We know that part of trauma is not only the pain and violence and shock of the event itself, but also the aftermath, and the ways in which the experience festers in the unsaid, the way it grows and morphs and digs in deeper.

Trauma survivors who are able to speak of what happened, who are believed, and who get support heal much faster than survivors who are locked into silence without support.

This may seem counterintuitive at first, but it makes perfect sense: Hemingway's story "The Snows of Kilimanjaro," in which a man on safari in Africa gets a small wound in his leg and then dies of gangrene because the wound goes untreated, is, I think, a perfect expression of what happens to our wounds if they are not tended to. It is no surprise that Hemingway was a trauma survivor: he implicitly knew the death sentence of living with an untreated wound.

To heal, we need to be able to listen to the body, recognize our wounds, and treat them.

This process takes time. It's messy. We need to grieve and mourn. We need to bring mind and body together. We need to speak and to feel.

We cannot rush this process.

Trauma inherently breaks the full scope of verbal language, and sometimes simple language can feel as if it dishonors the complexity and horror of the lived experience of trauma. And yet, if we don't put our experiences into language to hear ourselves and feel ourselves heard by others, our trauma will continue to circulate within us silently and distress us.

The more that I listened to myself and my body, developed self-compassion, found supports, and put into language what had happened to me so that I could connect with others, the better I felt.

I stopped having panic attacks. The parasite did not come back.

The cost of trauma is high—this violent, unnamed, unacknowledged event that happened when I was a very small child cast a shadow over much of my life and almost killed me several times over.

But if trauma and silence stole things from me, healing also brought me new connections—with myself, with my body, with others, and with the spiritual realm.

As I brought mind and body together, at that place of intersection, I found a little window into something boundless, and to my surprise, full of peace.

I discovered that on the other side of violence, strangely, almost inexplicably, was not more horror but peace.

I had been so worried that in looking directly at my trauma, I would see and be caught by the utter horror of the world, but if the trauma itself was horrible, behind it,

I seemed to be able to touch a realm of real compassion, openness, gentleness, and love.

This realm, too, was nameless, beyond the logical mind and language, but this silence was not oppressive as the first was—instead it was expansive.

As I go about my daily life, I can, of course, lose touch with this peace, and I can be caught again by horror and suffering. But when I experience the realm of peace, it feels so right and true that I believe it is what so many different spiritual traditions point to and, in their different languages, call God or Buddha Nature or the One or just plain Love.

Reindeer Girls
Katie Simon

M Y FRIEND MATILDA is from above the Arctic Circle in Sweden. There are more reindeer there than people. When we met, 18 years old and staying in the same hostel in Tel Aviv, Israel, she told me a story about reindeer hunting: hooves trampling snow, sprinting away from men with guns.

Matilda the reindeer, I decided to call her: beautiful, wild, furious at being hunted. Some Swedish men hunted reindeer and reindeer-girls alike, prey to be bloodied. Four hundred pounds of steaming flesh, immensity on ice, shot down with bullets one ten-thousandth their weight; one hundred pounds of thin hot girl-woman, broken teeth and bruises hidden from her mother.

Matilda loved the woods where she played growing up, but the men who raped her in her small Swedish town lurked in those woods, too. So, as soon as she could, Matilda left the reindeer and the rapists and the pain. We had each boarded flights to Israel, her from Stockholm and me from Boston, the ink on our high school diplomas still wet. It was easier for us to abandon the places that held our pain and take on the world than to stay still.

Before I met Matilda, I hadn't yet found the language to describe the same-sex sexual assault I had endured a decade earlier. I bottled the stories up deep in my belly, convinced they could never be told, and put on a happy mask. Sometimes we can choose to be happy in the face of hardship, but for me, in this case, that choice was a farce, a disguise I wore for myself and others.

Matilda ripped off my mask with her matter-of-fact honesty, her ownership of the ways in which she had been violated, of the agency she had reclaimed, and of the targeted anger she had unleashed. There were no secrets buried in her belly, not from me.

Matilda saw the sister-likeness of us before I did. She was more in tune with her pain, and therefore with mine. When I met Matilda, I was drowning my pain in vodka, waterboarding it with both fists. Matilda orbited my pain, gravitated toward it, and went in for the kill, ripping it out of my belly with our desert screaming and our sidewalk crying and our nightly hurling of caution to the wind. She saved it from my suffocating clutch and helped me feel it. She bared her own pain so I could say "me, too," if not to her, then at least to myself, and eventually, to others.

There is something about being pain refugees, practically warriors, that bonds people. You can smell it on us, rage-perfume. Matilda and I took a road trip in the Negev Desert, scrambled onto the roof of our lime green rental car and screamed into the windy loud silence. Screamed until we scratched our own throats raw. We sat on Tel Aviv's sidewalks sometimes, telling each other the stories of the people who had hurt us and haunted us even today, though their hands had not attacked us for years. We got fuck-the-world drunk most nights we spent together just to shake off that molested-lonely-girl pain. We shared that particular brand of pain, but we would each have swallowed the loss of that bond if it meant being free of the ghost-violence of our pasts.

When we met, I had decided to call her Matilda the reindeer: beautiful, wild, furious at being hunted. I did not know then, could not have known then, that in naming her, I was naming myself. Reindeer girls, not girl. After witnessing Matilda's wildness, I set my own stories free into the world, and in doing so, I released a pain I had been holding onto for ten years.

Years later, I sat on another friend's porch, the Massachusetts November chill penetrating the tunnels of our nostrils and the ducts of our eyes, our silhouettes haloed by Christmas lights. I told him about a sexual assault from years before, just talking, just sharing. The act of speaking didn't bother me as it once would have. I had almost forgotten what it felt like to keep those stories bottled up inside me.

"You're so unreserved. It's unusual," he told me. I didn't get it.

"You don't mind talking about things other people won't talk about." He meant pain.

I learned that from Matilda.

Waterways
Aisha Fukushima

Is no body sacred?
Daughter of a maid,
but she couldn't clean this di/stain
that unnamed man left marked—
his injurious journey of pleasure,
no room for measure
of impact

Swimming,
suddenly the pool was hot with shame.
Kiddy laps
turned to time lapses in my brain,
replaying the moment again and again.

Give me a bath of epsom salt
to heal this pain.
His fingers entered places
they should not have felt,
playing cards that had no right to be dealt.

On the long ride home,
silence ensued;

heart singing;
vocal chords subdued;
my usual self was not in the mood
for conversation.

Traced the corners of my mind
for mistakes I've made,
but there were no right angles.
Trying to calculate how I brought it onto myself,
but the math just didn't add up.

It's a wonder that I finally spoke up—
words tumbled from my mouth like sand
parched by the touch of unnamed man.
"Mom" I whispered "is it okay that a stranger touched me
   there?"

Street lights traced the lines of her face,
steering wheel turned like tides
back to the place where the earth had run dry.
My eyes glazed,
harsh fluorescent light,
photos of gym members
who had passed through that night,
flash, flash, flashed across gray screen.
All the meanwhile,
I wished I could somehow wake up from this nightmarish
   dream.

And now,
over 20 years later,
I can still map the trauma lines on my body
like mini-battle fronts
that illuminate with fire
every time a man calls cat on the street.

Aisha Fukushima

A desperate attempt to not drown under the lead mask of
    masculinity
that gives not oxygen in this undertow
replete with toxicity,
basing power on oppression
suppression of the stories
that dwell in our skin.

I still visit the water sometimes,
and I speak to the ocean
for I know that it will understand.
And it will share my story with the mountains and rivers,
the seedlings and the grandma trees,
who will transform it all into fresh air.

And as I sip honey on the edge
where salt water and sand meet,
I am home.
And I look up to realize that I am not alone.
Like the sweet white and blue lines of the sea
I am still fantastically, dynamically me.

And as sure as the sun and the moon and the tides will
    profess,
the waters will return
for no energy is created or destroyed,
only transformed.
And over the roar of blue crests
and the tender secrets of the most quiet streams,
we will map the anatomy of silence
& weave healing oceanic dreams.

Ashe.
Ashe.
Ashe.

About Our Contributors

Cyra 'Perry' Dougherty is a space holder for the spiritual growth and healing of 21st century leaders. She is the founder and CEO of Rootwise Leadership, Senior Partner at Still Harbor, and an Instructor of Leadership Programming at the Harvard T.H. Chan School of Public Health.

Joan Kresich is a long-time public school educator now working to bring restorative justice and sustainable practices to her community. She is the author of *Picturing Restorative Justice*. Her poetry and prose have appeared in *Adanna Literary Journal, Chrysalis Reader, HeART Online, CounterPunch, Albatross*, and the *Ms. Magazine* blog, among others.

Melissa Dickey is the author of two books of poems, *Dragons* and *The Lily Will*, both from Rescue Press. She holds degrees from the University of Washington and the Iowa Writers' workshop. Her poetry, nonfiction, and reviews have appeared in *Puerto del Sol, Columbia Poetry Review, The Spectacle, The Laurel Review*, and *Kenyon Review Online*, among others.

Andrea Roach, a writer of memoir and essays, lives and works in Boston. She received her MFA from Lesley University. In 2016, Andrea was a finalist for The Writer's Room of Boston Fellowship Award. An essay Andrea wrote was shortlisted in *Memoir Magazine's* 2018 #MeToo Essay Contest. She's currently working on new essays and her first memoir about the blurred lines of love, family, and violence. Andrea's work has been featured in *Blavity* and *Under The Gumtree.*

Caroline Numuhire is Rwandan writer who was born in Butare and grew up in Kigali. She is the author of *Mirror Of Stolen Hearts,* a collection of short stories and *L'Oncle gynécologue,* a French novel. This year, she was the contributing author to *Redemption Song and Other Stories,* the 2018 Caine Prize for African Writing Anthology. As an agricultural technician, she has worked for philanthropic organizations with the mission of improving livelihoods.

Esther Diplock, (B Occ Thy, M Couns) is a Gender Equity and Reconciliation International (GERI) Facilitator and Program Coordinator, based in Brisbane, Australia. She is an Individual & Couple Therapist, Educator, and Supervisor, specializing in Body Psychotherapy and trauma–informed practice. She is in private practice and lectures in tertiary institutions.

Chelsea MacMillan s an activist, spiritual director, writer, facilitator, and Co-Founder & Director of Brooklyn Center for Sacred Activism. Chelsea co-hosts *The Rising: Spirituality for Revolution*, a podcast for sacred activists, and her writing has appeared in *Anchor Magazine*, on Patheos. com, and in Matthew Fox's book *Order of the Sacred Earth*. Chelsea likes to sing showtunes, ride her bike around

Brooklyn, and geek out over the Enneagram. She is one half of the singing duo, LOON.

Pamela Bettencourt is a registered nurse, an entrepreneur, and a survivor of child sexual abuse. She uses writing as a therapy, but with the support of Laura van den Berg, an American author and English lecturer, she focused on using her writings as a tool to educate society and help sexual abuse victims heal and feel less stigmatized.

Patrick McFarlane is the Director of Behavioral Medicine at a Family Medicine Residency. Training in social work, psychology, and nursing inspired his areas of research interest focused around the use of phenomenology, narrative, and art to better understand his patients and develop effective interventions to address violence in primary care.

Monique Harris serves as a Senior Partner at Still Harbor, supporting the organization's work in social justice chaplaincy. A public educator for more than 17 years, she is also an ordained minister, formerly serving the African Methodist Episcopal Church. Though no longer teaching, Monique continues to exercise her passion for education via literacy and educational advocacy.

Jennifer Jean's debut poetry collection is *The Fool* (Big Table, 2013). Her chapbooks include: *In the War* and *The Archivist*. She's received a 2018 Disquiet FLAD Fellowship, and a 2017 "Her Story Is" residency to collaborate in Dubai with Iraqi women artists. Her work has appeared in: *Poetry Magazine, Rattle, Waxwing, Crab Creek Review*, and more. Jennifer is Managing Editor of *Talking Writing*, Co-Director of Morning Garden Artists Retreats, and Director of Free2Write Poetry Workshops for trauma survivors.

Amna Abdullatif is a community psychologist currently working as the national lead on children and young people for a leading national domestic violence charity in the UK. She has spent the last 10 years working with women and children within the voluntary sector for a range of organisations and is particularly interested in exploring women and children's agency, empowerment and the ability to engage in social action and change.

Lauren Spahn is a social justice advocate. She practices as a freelance writer, yoga teacher and doula supporting justice-based organizations. She also serves as lead administrator, facilitator and chaplain in her role as Senior Partner with Still Harbor. Lauren brings an insightful perspective on gender justice informed by her holistic experiences in women's health. She stays tethered to her call to bring people together through shared dialogue and practice and, in doing so, has discovered the healing and transformative power of community.

Michelle Bowdler's writing has been seen in the *Brevity Blog, Burningword Journal, Gertrude Press, The Rumpus*, and other literary magazines. She has been published in the *New York Times* and has two essays *We Rise to Resist: Voices from a New Era in Women's Political Action*, which won two international book awards. She is a recipient of the Barbara Deming Memorial Fund Award for Non-Fiction, a GrubStreet Memoir Incubator Alum, and was a Fellow at Ragdale Writers Colony and MacDowell Colony

Ashley Easter is an author, speaker, and abuse-victim advocate who educates churches and secular communities on abuse, safe practices, and effective resources. Ashley founded The Courage Conference, a survivor-centered movement focused on self-healing to empower victims to discover their courage and reclaim their freedom through connection, learning, and advocacy. She is the author of *The Courage Coach: A Practical, Friendly Guide on How to Heal From Abuse* and *Cults: Hidden in Plain Sight.*

Frederick Marx is an Academy- and Emmy-nominated filmmaker (*Hoop Dreams*) who has worked 35 years in film and television, creating stories that transform lives. *Journey from Zanskar* features the Dalai Lama and Richard Gere. His feature film *The Unspoken*, his documentary mini-series *Boys to Men?*, and *Rites of Passage* all express deep concerns about teen boys realizing mature masculinity. He is the authors of *At Death Do Us Part*, and he is currently in production on *Veterans Journey Home.*

Amy Elizabeth Paulson is a compassionate warrior, healing activist, and co-founder of Gratitude Alliance, an organization dedicated to transforming individual and collective trauma into healing, resilience, and self-empowerment for communities around the world. A Korean adoptee and survivor of trauma and sexual abuse, Amy is on a lifelong journey to seek joy, laughter, and profound connection even in the darkest of times.

Emily Porth is a storyteller, pilgrim, and ecofeminist. She trained as a cultural anthropologist prior to completing an interdisciplinary doctorate in Environmental Studies (York University). Her passion for social change inspired her to pursue storytelling as a medium for connecting with others and encouraging them to see the world differently. Emily currently spends most of her time writing, coordinating a Druid grove, visiting sacred sites, and cuddling cats.

Terrence 'Red' Crowley was born in Missouri and raised in the southeast US (Louisiana, Mississippi, and Alabama) to his working class parents who did exactly that to put him through college. In 1970 he earned a Master's Degree in psychology and went on to work for Vocational Rehabilitation. For the past 30 years, he has worked with himself and other men to create safety and justice for women.

Khalisa Rae is the author of *Real Girls Have Real Problems* (Sable Books, 2012). Her recent work appears in *Requiem Magazine*, *Dirty Chai*, and *Tishman Review*, among others. She is a finalist in the Furious Flower Gwendolyn Brooks Prize and a winner of the Fem Lit Magazine Contest. She is a former staff editor of the *Qu Lit Mag*, Creative Director of Athenian Press, and is currently finalizing her full-length poetry book, *Outside the Canon: Poetry as Protest.*

stephen hicks is funkier than a mosquito's tweeter. He's energetic, poetic, athletic, and has good credit. A benevolent king of the dancefloor who can teach you how to dougie and do the humpty dance. He also has several degrees: an ABS from Virginia Commonwealth University in Journalism, African-American Studies, and Political science; and a MPH from George Mason University in Global Health.

Steven Strafford is an actor and playwright who lives in Chicago with his husband, Wade. As an actor, he has worked around the country and the world, on stage and on screen. Steven is the author and performer of the award-winning, critically-acclaimed show, *Methtacular!,* which has toured from Maine to California. He is the author of several plays that are receiving productions around the country, including *Small Jokes About Monsters*, *Mona Q: Age 38*, and *The Breakup Play.*

Alandra Markman is a starseed from the 8th dimension of the Antares system who is here to assist Earth ascension. He is a spiritual guide, poet, musician, and dancer currently based in New York City and New Orleans. He is a multi-disciplinary improviser, healer, and composer. His Poetry Upon Request project has provided over 10,000 patrons with improvised poems at a typewriter. He is a survivor of incest and trafficking by his mother.

Nadia Colburn is the Founder of Align Your Story, writing classes and coaching. Nadia holds a PhD from Columbia and a BA from Harvard, and is a yoga teacher, student of Thich Nhat Hanh, activist and mother. Her writing appears in over 70 publications including *The New Yorker, The Boston Globe Magazine, Yes! Spirituality & Health*, and elsewhere.

Katie Simon's writing has appeared or is forthcoming in *The New York Times, Longreads, Lenny, The Lily, The Rumpus, Brevity, Health, BuzzFeed, Entropy, Ravishly, BUST, Women's Health, Hippocampus*, and more. She is working on a memoir about the year she contracted the plague bacteria, was raped by a stranger in an alleyway, and found herself in Cairo during the Egyptian Revolution.

Aisha Fukushima is a singer, speaker, educator, and 'RAPtivist' (rap activist). Fukushima founded RAPtivism (Rap Activism), a hip hop project spanning 20 countries and four continents, amplifying universal efforts for freedom and justice. She is a multilingual, multiracial African American Japanese woman who lectures and performs worldwide. Fukushima's 'RAPtivism' work has been featured via *Oprah Magazine*, TEDx, KQED Public Television, *The Seattle Times*, TV 2M Morocco, *The Bangalore Mirror, HYPE* and others.

Our Thanks Goes To...

We are indebted joyfully to our backers, whose support helped us to show up loud and proud with this book. To those named below, and to the countless others that prefer to remain nameless, we are grateful.

Adrian Sell and Kate Wareing, Audrey Schwartz, Alastair Horne, Alexa Dougherty, Allison van Zyl, Amy Elizabeth Paulson, Andréa Fernandes, Angel and Philip Buchanan, Ann Hardt Williams, April Fenton, Babita Patel, Barbara Greaves, Barney, Barry Goddard, Beth and Tim Rockcress, Bobby McGill, C. Axtmayer, Candace Coakley, Carolyn Gilman, Carolyn Smith, Cassandra Goldwater, Catriona M Cox, Ceci Foster, Charlotte and Dick Dougherty, Chelsea Pashen, Cher-Wen DeWitt, Chiara Bullen, Chris Townson, Christina B Dupin, Christina Kopp, Christopher Hamon, Claire Hodgson, Cyra Perry Dougherty. David and Sandra Knotts, David McArdle, Debbie Okrina, Debbie Prior, Debby Schlein, Devin Green, Dominique, Elyssa Pompa, Emily Ausubel, Emily Rowles, Emma Post, Emmie Harrison, Erica Charis, Erin Donovan and Dr. Barbara Russell, Esther Diplock, Ewan Mackie and Valerie Porth, Finbarr Farragher, Floraidh, Gail Offen-Brown,

Gratitude Alliance, Hannah Bloczynski, Heidi Engstrom Tessmer, Holly McKenna, Ian Warthin, Janet Bednarz, Jay Aquinas Thompson and Caitlin Rippey, Jayne Herring, Jeff Spahn, Jennifer Constable, Jennifer Perry, Jenny Wagner, Jo Gabrielle Ripoll, Jodi Collett, John and Yvette Roddy, Joshia, Julia Fitzgerald and Karen Gorst, Karina Hathaway, Kate Shugert, Kate Thorson, Kate Webber and Jo Webber, Katherine Knotts, Katie Smith, Kristin Folk, Kristin Lager Morse, L Cairns, Laura K Lee Dellinger, Lauren Galinsky, Laurie Dougherty, Laurie Racicot, LeeAnn Mallorie, Linda Smith, Lisa and Barry Fireman, Lisa Elkins, Lonna Mathie, Louisa Burden, Lydia, Mariah Breeding, Mark and Nikki Vinckier, Mark W Moran (LCSW), Matthew Diovatelli, Melissa Merres, Melissa Smith, Melody A. Kramer (Legal Greenhouse), Michael Stallings, Michele O'Brien, Mika Cook, Monica R. Weltzien, Monique Hill, Morse Michelle, Nadia Colburn, Nancy Gagnon-Jutras, Nicole Weiler, Odenkirk C. Dandies, P. Cochrane, Patrick S. McFarlane, Patty Simon, Paul Henshall, Perry H E Carrison, Peter Butler, Rick Foot, Rita Wuebbeler, Robbie Gamble, Ross Sayers, Sarah Marsh, Sarah McFadden and Monica Logan, Shane Snowdon, Shaw Flick, Sheila Davis, Sheridan Katy, Sherry Yu, Sheryle Gillihan, Silvia Molina, So Yoon (Yoonie) Sim, Sonia Cottrell, Stevie Marsden, Susan McGee Bailey, Suzi Rutti, Tim Delong Jr and Heidi Keller, Toby Millard, Tony Edwards, Tony Sheldon, Tyrell Kumlin, Vanessa Sage (PhD), Vicki Stephens, Vix Hobbs.

red